THE WONDER-WORKING
POWER OF GOD

THE WONDER-WORKING POWER OF GOD

Cornelia Addington

DeVorss & Company, Publishers
P.O. Box 550—Marina del Rey—California 90294

ISBN: 0-87516-589-3
Library of Congress Card Catalog Number: 87-70231

Cover design by Don Farmer.
Spiritual photography by Dick Canby,
of Canby's Camera, Box 4260,
Sedona West, AZ 86340.
Phone: (602) 282-2069

Printed in the United States of America

TABLE OF CONTENTS

PREFACE

God works in mysterious ways, His wonders to perform, declares a beautiful old hymn. The Father has so many ways to bless us when we turn our lives over to Him.

Our daily mail constantly brings letters from people bemoaning the fact that they cannot "find God" or have become "separated from God." No one can see God. We know him through His wondrous works. We feel Him moving in our lives. He speaks to us as we are able to receive Him, in ways we can accept. Sometimes our answers come dramatically in the headline of a newspaper; sometimes we pick up a magazine and there is the answer we sought staring at us from an article we were led to read. At another time, a trusted friend may telephone us with just the words we needed to hear; or, like a burst of light, the Guidance comes from within, intuitively. We recognize it for what it is with a glad feeling of reassurance. *Lo, I am with you always. . . . I will not leave you, nor forsake you.*

The Wonder-working Power reaches each one of us at our own point of awareness. To some, it is given to experience what the world would call a miracle; others feel the Presence at work in their lives through everyday experiences. This book is designed to give the reader a realization of the Power and an understanding of some of the many ways It can work in our lives.

The Wonder-working Power of God has always been known to the illumined of the ages. It is constantly being rediscovered in a fresh, vital way by the individual.

The spiritual journey is an exciting adventure. One may have many teachers along the way, but always the right teacher is there when needed. There is an old saying that is proved over and over again: "When the student is ready, the teacher appears." Sometimes the "teacher" is in written form; sometimes it is a person. Then again, the "teacher" takes the form of a dream or a powerful waking thought. But always, it is the lesson needed at that very moment. *Truth, by whomsoever spoken, is from God.*

Part I of this book is designed to provide an understanding of the Wonder-working Power of God, ever available to us.

Part II describes some of the ways the Power manifests in our daily lives.

May you find within these pages the inspiration that you seek today, and may your search for Truth never end.

CORNELIA ADDINGTON

PART I

REALIZING THE
WONDER-WORKING POWER

Open thou mine eyes, that I may behold
wondrous things out of thy law.
—Psalm 119:18

1

CHRIST, THE POWER
THAT DWELLS IN YOU

---

*Now we have received, not the spirit of the world, but
the spirit which is of God; that we might know the
things that are freely given to us of God.*

—1 Cor. 2:12

Within each one of us there is a Power so great that
we cannot begin to conceive of It. Without an awareness of this Power we are helpless. With It, all things
are possible. If we have thought of ourselves as inadequate to meet the challenges of life, it is only because
we had mistakenly believed that we had become separated from the Power.

JESUS, THE CHRIST

Jesus identified himself so completely with the Power of God within that he became known as the Christ. *With men this is impossible*, he said. *But with God all things are possible.*[1] He called the Power that he knew so intimately, *Father*. He accepted the fact that *the Father* was able to do all things through him. To the world, these mighty works seemed to be miracles. To Jesus, they were perfectly natural and understandable. The Wisdom within provided the answers. The Love within healed and blessed all who came into his presence. He explained it this way: *The Father within me doeth the works.*[2]

Jesus knew that God lived through him but he accepted this awesome idea for us, too. He said that all that he did we could do also, and even greater things could we do.[3] He believed that each one expressed God at his own level of awareness. Can we believe this? Can we accept this knowledge as our greatest treasure? If so, it can be the substance of our every desire, the answer to our every need.

Whereas Jesus referred to *the Father that doeth the works*[4] and *the kingdom of God within*,[5] Paul spoke of *the*

1. Matt. 19:26.
2. John 14:10.
3. John 14:12.
4. John 14:12.
5. Luke 17:21.

4

exceeding grace of God in you[6] and, in a moment of high exultation, exclaimed: *Thanks be to God for his unspeakable gift.*[7] Both Jesus and Paul were speaking of the Christ, which is God individualized in and through man, God expressing in us.

WE MUST DISCOVER THE POWER WITHIN OURSELVES

Can we accept the *unspeakable gift* for ourselves? Can we accept *Christ in us, the hope of glory?*[8] Christ is the evidence of the Almighty Power of God that we embody as the attributes of God, all that God stands for. As someone once said, "That little three-letter word includes so much." God in us is Spirit, Love, Life, Truth, Wisdom, Power, and Intelligence. It is the Power that doeth the works.

Every problem we have ever experienced has come from a sense of separation from God within. Therefore, every healing must come from a realization of our oneness with God.

Thou art the Christ, the son of the living God,[9] said Peter to Jesus. Too often we have accepted the Christ for Jesus but not for ourselves. We must find the Power in

6. 2 Cor. 9:14.
7. 2 Cor. 9:15.
8. Col. 1:27.
9. Matt. 16:16.

5

ourselves before we can demonstrate it in our lives. Christ within is our perfect health. All who touch the hem of his garment (all those who realize their true spiritual perfection) are made whole. Let us know this for ourselves that we may be made whole.

MEDITATION

The wholeness of God is my health and my well-being. In the Mind of God where I live and move and have my being, there is a divine proto-type, a perfect pattern for the perfect being that I am. Physical imperfection drops away as I recognize my true Self. In the degree that I am able to realize the wholeness and perfection of Christ within me, I am made whole. All who cross my path are restored by my awareness of the perfect Life of God within me. Christ in me is my perfect health.

And so it is.

2

THE UNSPEAKABLE GIFT

Thanks be unto God for his unspeakable gift.
—2 Cor. 9:15

Sometimes a word, understood, makes all the difference. The words of Paul to the Corinthians return to my mind again and again: *Thanks be unto God for his unspeakable gift!*[1]

"What did he mean by unspeakable?" I wondered. Finally, I looked the word up in my dictionary and discovered that *unspeakable* means *incapable of being described; indescribable; that which cannot be expressed.* Here was food for thought.

Paul tried to explain it. He called it a *free gift;*[2] the

1. 2 Cor. 9:15.
2. Rom. 5:15, 18.

heavenly gift;[3] *the gift of God;*[4] *the gift by Grace;*[5] and he cautioned us to *neglect not the gift that is in thee.*[6]

What is this gift that cannot be described? It is *Christ in you the hope of glory;* it is *the kingdom of God within you;* it is *the Spirit of God that dwelleth in you;*[7] it is the greatest gift of all *that we should be called the sons of God.*[8]

THE INFINITE CANNOT BE DESCRIBED

Truly it is indescribable, for who can describe the Almighty? The Infinite is beyond man's concept, yet the gift of the Infinite, with all that it includes, is hidden within each one of us. Who can describe infinite Love, eternal Life, all-Knowledge, and never-ending Beauty? Who can conceive of the omnipresence of God of which we are, each one of us, the individual expression? The gift is so far-reaching that it boggles the mind, yet it is free. All that is asked of us is that we accept it. No one is excluded. We are the sons of God; and, *if sons, then heirs, joint-heirs with Jesus Christ.* Paul had these wonderful moments of illumination that continue

3. Heb. 6:4.
4. Rom. 6:23.
5. 2 Cor. 9:8.
6. 1 Tim. 4:14.
7. John 14:17.
8. 1 John 3:1.

to light up the Spirit within us whenever we remember them.

> *For as many as are led by the Spirit of God, they are the sons of God.*
>
> *For ye have not received the spirit of bondage again to fear; but ye have received the Spirit of adoption, whereby we cry, Abba, Father.*
>
> *The Spirit itself beareth witness with our spirit, that we are the children of God:*
>
> *And if children, then heirs; heirs of God, and joint-heirs with Christ.*[9]

IT IS ALL OURS FOR THE ASKING

All this has been given to us. And, as James Russell Lowell wrote in *The Vision of Sir Launfal*:

> *'Tis heaven alone that is given away,*
> *'Tis only God may be had for the asking.*

The moment we are willing to partake of the *unspeakable gift*, we are like the prodigal son returning to the Father's house—the Father comes out to meet us. Where there was darkness in the soul, now the Light is come; if we were sorrowful, depressed, or gloomy, now Joy breaks through again; loneliness is no more,

9. Rom. 8:14–17.

for the Son is companioned by the Spirit. We are the *sons of the living God*, and the inheritance is all ours. *All that the Father hath is thine*[10] was a promise for us!

Do you know that you celebrate the Christ every time you have a glimpse of yourself as the perfect child of God you are? Every time you say, "Our Father," you accept all men as brothers, making you part of the Oneness of God, the unity of all of Life. Every time Love conquers criticism and discontent within your heart; every time you make peace with another, no matter what he has done to you; every time you let the Christ Light shine for someone who has not yet discovered God within himself, you prove the Master who said *ye are the light of the world*.[11]

Nothing is worth fretting over; nothing is worth letting ourselves become separated from the joyous Spirit of God within; nothing can dim the Light unless we let it. Let that Light shine for all the world to see. *Arise and shine; for thy light is come, and the glory of the Lord is risen upon thee*.[12] The Christ Light is *your hope of glory*: your hope of a glorious new life, replete with the *freedom of the sons of God*. Never again need you sit in the darkness, for the Light shines in the darkest places so that the *night shineth as the day*[13] and there is no place where God is not when you know He is in you. This is the gift of God!

10. Luke 15:31.
11. Matt. 5:14.
12. Is. 60:1.
13. Ps. 139:12.

RECOGNIZING THE GIFTS OF GOD

Now we have received, Paul tells us, *not the spirit of the world, but the spirit which is of God; that we might know the things that are freely given to us of God.*[14]

What are some of the things so freely given to us of God? When we meditate, it is well to dwell upon the attributes of God. These are the things so freely given to us, His offspring, His image and likeness, His dearly beloved.

God is—therefore we are.

What is it that God is and that we are?

The Bible tells us that *God is Love.*[15] Therefore, we are loving, we are understanding, compassionate, at peace with ourselves and with others. God is Love, and when we love, we partake of His nature; in loving, we let His Love live through us. It therefore behooves us to put aside all thoughts of resistance, all unloving thoughts, that we may express His image and likeness, letting His Love live through us. *We love because He first loved us.*[16] If it were not that Love was freely given to us of God, we could not love at all, for we would not know Love.

14. 1 Cor. 2:12.
15. 1 John 4:8.
16. 1 John 4:19.

MEDITATION

God is Love. I receive Love and let it express through me. I am a center in divine Love. I let it well up within me and consciously share it with my family, my friends, and all who need its blessing. Turning to those whom I would help, I think: "God is loving you through me, and His Love heals you of any sense of separation."

God is—therefore we are. We are His image and likeness, heirs to the kingdom of God; heirs to all of the wonderful things so freely given to us of God.

God is Peace; therefore we are filled with Peace. Instead of dwelling on the turmoil and chaos that seem to exist in the world, let us put them aside and put on the armor of Peace. Let us now receive the Peace so freely given to us of God.

MEDITATION

God is Peace; therefore I am filled with Peace. Turning to all those whom I would help, I give them my Peace, even as Jesus gave his Peace when he said: *My peace I give unto you, not as the world giveth, give I unto you.*[17] He gave of the Peace that he had received. I give of the Peace so freely given

17. John 14:27.

12

to me of God, the Peace that comes with knowing I am one with God.

After we have received our Peace and given it to
those in our immediate circle, it is well to move out into
the larger circle, giving our peace to all those who have
great need of it today, those who think that they are
frustrated, separated, insecure, troubled, and fright-
ened.* The Peace of God we now receive knows no op-
position, no resistance. It draws together all of Life.

God is Light, and in Him is no darkness at all.[18] Have
there seemed to be dark places in your thinking? By
receiving the gift of Light so freely given to us of God,
the darkness disappears. Where there was darkness,
now there is Light. The darkness is dissolved by the
Light as it illumines our pathway, giving us understanding. In the Light of divine Intelligence, there is no darkness at all. As a lamp glows in the darkness, we are
radiant with Light. It glows in our souls, our minds and
our bodies; even the cells in our bodies are made of
Light.

---

*For a thoroughgoing treatment of the significance and tech-
niques of extending our peace and love to those who need them—
including those we find hard to love or who may have despitefully
used us—see *Drawing the Larger Circle*, by Jack and Cornelia
Addington (Marina del Rey, Calif.: DeVorss & Co., 1985).

18. 1 John 1:5.

MEDITATION

God in me is Light, the Light upon my path.
Having received the gift of Light, I now turn to
those who need help and know for them: God in
you is Light, the Light that you seek, the Light
upon your path.

God is Truth, the Truth that sets us free.[19] Always,
when we are troubled, there is some Truth that is
needed. As we become receptive to the still, small voice
within, It teaches us all that we need to know, the very
Truth that we are needing. Truth dawns within us like
a bright new day and never again will we be the same.
This is *the Comforter* that Jesus promised, *even the spirit
of Truth*[20] that would teach us all that we needed to
know. This is the gift of God so freely given, teaching
us in that selfsame moment all that we need to do or
say.

These are the gifts that are freely given to us of God,
His very nature. He gives us of Himself—Love—
Light—Peace—Truth—that we might be His image.

MEDITATION

We thank Thee, Father, for all of Thy gifts. For
these and all of the blessings that we receive, we
are truly grateful.

19. John 8:32.
20. John 14:16, 17.

14

CHAPTER

3

THE GRACE OF GOD
IS ALL-INCLUSIVE

For the Lord is a sun and shield: the Lord will give grace and glory; no good thing will he withhold from them that walk uprightly.

—Ps. 84:11

And God is able to make all grace abound toward you; that ye, always having all sufficiency in all things, may abound to every good work.[1]

God is Love, illimitable Love in action, pouring Itself out without stint through all of creation. This is the meaning of Grace. Whenever we have a problem, it is because we are thinking of ourselves as mortals instead of the divine, perfect beings we really are.

God expresses through us. As divine beings, we are

---

1. 2 Cor. 9:8.

Love in action. Any problem, of any nature what-soever, is a sense of separation from the Love of God, the *Grace of God*, as it is called in the Bible. Healing oc-curs when unity or a sense of oneness with God is reestablished in consciousness.

GOD'S GRACE COVERS EVERY NEED

God is able to make all grace abound toward you. This is why healings, or "demonstrations," often come in bunches, a sort of "package unit." God's Grace is all-inclusive. It is not meted out in dribbles to the strictly deserving. The rain falls on the just and the unjust. The Grace of God is free to all those who will receive it, even in a measure. This perhaps explains a few puzzling things; such as, why healings often occur before the healing ministry or healing group has even received the request. The seeker has opened the door to God's Grace, and the illimitable Love has been quick to pour in. God's Love covers every need.

Love is the only substance. It is all that we need. It becomes every "commodity." Having an awareness of it in some measure is *always having all sufficiency in all things.*

Paul wrote as he glimpsed this Truth: *I besought the Lord . . . And He said unto me, my grace is sufficient for thee: for my strength is made perfect in weakness.*[2]

2. 2 Cor. 12:9.

The Grace of God becomes ideas and fresh inspiration to the writer, the speaker, the teacher. It is understanding, immediately available to those who have human relation adjustments to make. *The blind receive their sight, and the lame walk, the lepers are cleansed, and the deaf hear, the dead are raised up, and the poor have the gospel preached to them.*[3] Whatever we need to abound unto every good work is supplied by the Grace of God. If this boundless supply of heavenly substance has seemed to be denied us, it is simply because we have not acknowledged It as the one and only Source of our good. We have looked on the outside for our answers, stumbling aimlessly among the husks of outer symbols: remedies that in and of themselves have no power, friends that passed us by, health and wealth that seemed to elude us.

GRACE IS ALL THINGS TO ALL PEOPLE

God is able to make all grace abound toward you. Grace may come through the doctor, a check in the mail, or an unexpected call from a friend; but Grace is always from God. It is all things to all people. It is the Absolute stepped down into the relative experience. It is Good made manifest where we can see it and touch it and feel it.

In the beginning was the Word, and the Word was with

3. Matt. 11:5.

17

God, and the Word was God.[4] We may paraphrase those words of John: *In the beginning was the Word, and the Word was with Love (for God is Love), and the Word was Love. And the Word (of Love) was made flesh, and dwelt among us . . . full of Grace and Truth.*[5]

Grace comes first as an awareness in consciousness. The rest is "signs following," the "by-products of Love," you might say. Open the heart to receive the Love of God even in a measure and the results are astounding. It is *all Grace*, more than we dared ask or hope for. It is hope to the hopeless, friendship to the friendless, wholeness called health. It is knowledge and wealth and power—but first, it is Grace.

Many things today are made of plastic; it is poured into an infinite variety of molds, but first it is plastic. The color, the form, and the variety are added unto it to fit the need. So it is with the Grace of God, that invisible substance out of which everything is created.

If you have a problem, the answer is *all Grace*, abounding unto you right this moment.

MEDITATION

God is loving me now, He loves me with an everlasting Love that will not let me go. There has never been a time when I have been separated

4. John 1:1.
5. John 1:14.

from this Love. In the Father's house is all that I need and to spare. "Nearer is He than breathing and closer than hands and feet." All that I need is here within me right now, because God is here. He will never leave me or forsake me. I am one with the Love of God and nothing can stand in Love's way. Love is my sufficiency in all things.

And so it is.

4

THE AWARENESS OF
THE PRESENCE

But there is a spirit in man: and the inspiration of the Almighty giveth them understanding.

—Job 32:8

Truly, prayer work is the most rewarding work in the world. God does the work—His teachers and practitioners receive, for Him, the gratitude of many people. *The blessing of the Lord, it maketh rich, and He addeth no sorrow with it.*[1] How wonderful it is to witness these blessings, not receiving the credit for ourselves, but giving the credit to God.

1. Prov. 10:22.

THE PRESENCE SPEAKS TO US
IN SPECIAL WAYS

Answered prayer is not always concerned with things. The soul's experience lingers on in retrospect long after things are forgotten. I have on my desk a beautiful letter from which I quote with the writer's permission:

One early morning just before dawn, I got up to walk in my garden, trying to rid myself of fears that seemed to come from all sides. I went downstairs, started the coffeemaker, and sat down to pray for faith and understanding of the great Love of God I know to be always present. Try as I would, peace would not come; so I decided to go outside and work in the soil. It was just beginning to grow light as I opened the sliding glass door onto the patio. The scent of orange blossoms was simply overpowering. I walked over to the tree and saw the first blossoms beginning to come forth. As I examined the small, white flower with the yellow center, contrasting so beautifully against the shiny green leaves, I wondered how anything so small could smell so wonderful. Standing there, I remembered one of the lectures Dr. Jack had given, his opening words . . . "I am aware, I am having a love affair with Life!" I had understood what he meant at the time; but here, standing in the early morning light of a new day, the words had even a deeper meaning.

I drew on my gardening gloves and knelt beside the long line of hibiscus bushes separating our property from our next-door neighbor. I began raking the dead leaves with my hands into a neat pile and suddenly became aware of having company. A large bluejay had hopped within six inches of my hands and was standing there looking at me. I had heard that these birds could easily be tamed, but I had never tried, and this bird could not have known me. I sat back on my heels and said, "Well, good morning." Immediately, he hopped over to me and gave my knee a sharp peck or two. I was thrilled. Never had I been so close to a wild bird before. I talked to him softly and he answered me with a series of clucks deep in his throat, all the time cocking his head from side to side and looking at me with sharp little eyes. Even after I started working again with the leaves, he stayed close to my hands, talking away. It was a most wonderful experience. Somehow I felt that this was meant to mean something special to me—and it did.

As I opened the door to go back into the house, the fresh, wonderful smell of coffee came on a wave from the kitchen. As I poured myself the first cup of morning coffee, I knew again what it meant to be aware. Glancing out of the window, I saw a strand of our beautiful Sunset Orange bougainvillea flowering vine blowing gently in the early morning air. It almost seemed to be nodding to me, and who can say that it wasn't! My husband's shout from upstairs wanting to know if breakfast was ready stirred me from my reverie; but then again I was aware of the blessing of having someone to get breakfast for, a good husband, and a grand companion.

Oh, those golden moments when we are aware of the Presence of God! Who are we to doubt that He who made the bluejay could not also send this bright messenger to bring His Love and blessing!

St. Paul told the Corinthians that he *preached Christ, the power and the wisdom of God.*[2] And then he spoke to the Colossians of the mystery *which is Christ in you, the hope of glory.*[3] It must have pleased Jesus to see that Paul, at least, had understood his message; that Christ, the power of God, lived in and through each one of us and was able to do all things for us, through us. The God Power, being omnipresent, does nothing *for* us, but is able to do everything *through* us.

CHRIST IN YOU IS POWER— CAN YOU ACCEPT IT?

When we feel confident, capable, able to meet the challenges of life successfully, we are happy and poised. When we allow ourselves to become discouraged, weak, and ineffective, we are miserable. If we depend solely upon the frail, human self, our spirits rise and fall. One day we may be on top, the next day we are down; problems seem gigantic and the human self inadequate to meet them. And all the time there is in us the Power to which nothing is impossible, that *unspeakable gift,* the Power of Almighty God living through us!

Jesus, the man who lived the Christ and proved the Christ, gave us the answer when he said, *With men it*

2. 1 Cor. 1:23, 24.

is impossible, but not with God: for with God all things are possible. Those who have believed him have had miraculous healings and have overcome seemingly impossible situations. Can you claim the Omnipotent Power for yourself? Try it. Affirm for yourself:

Christ in me is power, power to meet every situation in my life. I can say with Jesus, *all power is given to me in heaven* [the divine within] *and earth* [the outer manifestation].[4]

Down through the ages, there were those who felt the Presence with them at all times. Joshua was one of them. He told the people: *Be strong and of a good courage, be not afraid, neither be thou dismayed: for the Lord thy God is with thee whithersoever thou goest.*[5]

CHRIST IN YOU IS YOUR PROTECTION

Fear is the greatest enemy of mankind. That is why it has been said by several great men, *There is nothing to fear but fear itself.* So many things in today's world seem to foster fear. It is, therefore, incumbent on us to develop an absolute conviction of divine protection for ourselves and others. Then, wherever we go, we can turn within and hear the still, small voice assure us: *Be strong and of a good courage; be not afraid, neither be thou*

3. Col. 1:27.
4. Matt. 28:18.
5. Josh. 1:9.

dismayed: for the Lord thy God is with thee withersoever thou goest—as I was with Moses, so I will be with thee: I will not fail thee, nor forsake thee.[6]

How was Moses protected? He had constant Guidance, a cloud by day and a pillar of fire by night; water appeared at the touch of his rod; manna provided all that was needed. When he led the children of Israel to the river, the waters divided to let them pass through. So it is with us. *When thou passest through the waters, I will be with thee; and through the rivers, they shall not overflow thee—fear not for I am with thee.*[7] The Christ within us is our protection always. Nothing can hurt us when we know:

MEDITATION

I am the dearly beloved of the Father. The Christ within me will never leave me or forsake me. I am protected always.

And so it is.

6. Josh. 1:5.
7. Isa. 43:2.

CHAPTER

5

HEAVEN AND EARTH ARE FULL OF THEE

That they should seek the Lord, if haply they might feel after him, and find him, though he be not far from every one of us: for in him we live and move and have our being.

—Acts 17:27, 28

Heaven and Earth are full of Thee, O Lord most high. I can still hear the choirs of my childhood making the rafters ring. In memory, my spirit soars again. I feel the old surge of mystic uplift, the stirring of the heart as the organ swells into its final crescendo, the choir's last note of high exultation. Replaying the music on the tape recorder of my mind, I find again the awareness of long ago. But, now I ask myself, "Do we really know what these inspiring words mean?"

26

Jesus, the man, lived 2000 years ago; but heaven and earth are still filled with Thee, the Christ that can never die; eternal God that can never be submerged; Emmanuel, God with us! O, *Thou Son of God, Thou only art the Truth!*

WE ARE THE PLACE WHERE GOD SHINES THROUGH

God works through us. It is happening today. It can happen through you *if you are willing to let it.* We are the place where God shines through. God needs you and me to accomplish His great work today. A recognition of "heaven and earth are full of Thee" can dissolve what seems to be wickedness in high places, can set the captive free and transform this troubled world into a paradise on earth.

UP, UP, AND AWAY!

Every time I travel by plane, as the plane takes off and lifts up into the air, I repeat to myself these beautiful words from the 139th Psalm:

> *Whither shall I go from thy spirit?*
> *or whither shall I flee from thy presence?*
> *If I ascend up into heaven, thou art there:*
> *if I make my bed in hell, behold, thou art there.*

If I take the wings of the morning,
   and dwell in the uttermost parts of the sea;
Even there shall thy hand lead me,
   and thy right hand shall hold me.[1]

My husband likes to tease me about this practice of mine. He says that the pilot should really be aware what a big help I am in getting that plane off the ground! I laugh with him, for I don't mind. It gets *me* off the ground spiritually, and that's worth a lot to me. The 139th Psalm gives me the feeling of the omnipresence of God every time.

There is absolutely nowhere we can go that God is not, for Spirit is everywhere present at the same time. Yes, even when we make our bed in hell, He is there, and this realization lifts us right out of the difficulty, no matter how dreadful it seems.

OMNIPRESENCE

(A Meditation on the 139th Psalm)

Whither shall I go from Thy Spirit?
  Whither *can* I go from Thy Spirit? Thou art "nearer than breathing, closer than hands or feet," for Thou art my very Life, the Intelligence that thinks through me, the Power that works in me,

1. Ps. 139: 7–10.

the Substance made manifest as me. Thou art all. Whither can I go from Thy Spirit?

Or whither shall I flee from Thy presence?

Whither *can* I flee from Thy presence? Thou art everywhere present. Thy love surrounds and keeps me. Thou art loving me through everyone and everything. Thy Love is everywhere present. *Whither can I flee from Thy presence?*

If I ascend up into heaven, Thou art there . . .

If I ascend up into a high state of consciousness where I abide in the Kingdom of Heaven within; of course, Thou art there, for in this awareness I am aware of Thee and Thee alone, but . . .

If I make my bed in hell, behold Thou art there . . .

Yes, even if I choose to separate myself from Thy omnipresent Love, asleep to Thy blessings, ignorant of Thy Truth, willfully flaunting my little human ego as I struggle with the separateness of personality and false appearances; behold, *Thou art there.* Right in the midst of my self-imposed misery, *Thou art there.* If I pause and turn in the slightest degree to Thy Wholeness, if I remember that in my Father's house there is enough and to spare, You come to meet me and welcome me Home again.

If I take the wings of the morning, and dwell in the uttermost parts of the sea . . .

Should I go off on some flight of fancy, drifting in a sea of thought to a far country, I find that Thou art there before me, filling all consciousness. Even the winds and the waves of thought obey Thee. Thou makest the sea to be calm, and . . .

Even there shall Thy hand lead me, and Thy right hand shall hold me. If I say, Surely the darkness shall cover me . . .

In the darkness of my human thinking when clouds of negation seem to cover me until I see no way out, just a little turning to Thy Truth, just a little leaning in Thy direction and . . .

Even the night shall be light about me. Yea, the darkness hideth not from Thee; but the night shineth as the day: the darkness and the light are both alike to Thee.

Thou art ever present. There is no Life but Thy Life. There is no Power but Thy Power. Whither can I go from Thy Spirit? Thou art all there is. I trust in Thee.

And so it is.

6

THE SPIRIT OF TRUTH
IS OUR GUIDE

*Howbeit when he, the Spirit of truth, is come, he will
guide you into all truth.*

—John 16:13

"Oh, if only someone would tell me what I should
do!"

As I read this woman's letter, I could feel her desper-
ation. Probably, she had already asked all of her
friends, and some of her enemies, what to do, and still
no satisfactory answers. Now she was writing us asking for prayer help. At last, she was on the right track.

DIVINE GUIDANCE IS ALWAYS AVAILABLE

Human advice is apt to be worthless, but there is Someone who can tell us what to do. The all-knowing Someone can see around the corners and can be counted on to give us trustworthy advice. Unfortunately, most of us wait until all other possibilities are exhausted before asking for divine Guidance.

But there is a spirit in man: and the inspiration of the Almighty giveth them understanding.[1]

As Job found, the guidance our friends give us is colored by their own past mistakes and human judgments. "I tried it once and it didn't work for me" may not be your experience at all. There is a right and perfect solution to your problem, and infinite Intelligence knows what it is. Divine Guidance can be trusted. You can trust it not to betray you.

THE SPIRIT OF TRUTH WILL SPEAK TO US IN MANY WAYS

When you turn to the inner Wisdom, the answer you are seeking will be given to you. It may come to you in some surprising way; perhaps a headline in a newspaper or a line in a novel you have been reading, or a stray remark that you will hear entirely out of context may lead you to your answer. You may find that you are

1. Job 32:8.

awakened out of a sound sleep with a brilliant idea. But when your Guidance comes, you will know it for what it is. You will know and *know* that you know. You will feel right about this Guidance. There will be no uncertainty in your mind when the true answer comes.

Again and again, the Bible promises to give us the Wisdom we seek:

If any of you lack wisdom, let him ask of God, that giveth to all men liberally and upbraideth not; and it shall be given him.[2]

Yes, it shall be given you in that same hour what ye shall speak. For it is not ye that speak but the Spirit of your Father which speaketh in you.[3]

And thine ears shall hear a word behind thee, saying, this is the way, walk ye in it, when ye turn to the right hand, and when ye turn to the left.[4]

THERE IS A BETTER WAY

How many times I have longed to tell another person what to do! It seemed so obvious to me, especially when the growth at hand was something I had experienced myself. Then I would bite my tongue and remind myself, there is a better way.

My personal advice would be based on human judgment, but the Spirit within my friend would give him

2. James 1:5.
3. Matt. 10:19, 20.
4. Isa. 30:21.

33

the Truth. Spiritual Guidance alone can be trusted. When Jesus knew he was leaving them, he promised his disciples that the Comforter would come, *even the Spirit of Truth. Howbeit when he, the Spirit of Truth, is come, he will guide you into all truth.*[5]

My prayer for another must be a recognition of the Spirit of Truth within him that can be counted on to tell him all that he needs to know for divine right action to take place.

Do you know what happens? Invariably, the Guidance comes, and the one I longed to help calls or writes to say, "It came to me like a light shining in the darkness that I should do such and such, or that I should say such and such." The clarification has come, and joyously, without my having to intrude my human judgment into the matter. When the Spirit of Truth gives the answer, there is no resistance and, miraculously, everyone is on the right track.

What a lot of useless worry we would save if we could always remember to ask the Teacher within what to do! Not to mention time saved asking our friends for advice. It took me many years to reach the point where I could trust my inner Guidance, but now I know for sure that there is One who knows. When I turn to Him, the answers come so easily that it never ceases to amaze me.

It shall be told thee what thou must do.[6]

5. John 16:13.
6. Acts 9:6.

MEDITATION

I trust the Spirit of Truth within me to tell me all that I need to know or do or say. The Wisdom within me knows what is for my highest good in this situation. When I cease looking to the outer and trust my Inner Guidance, I am directed into paths of right action.

I trust the Spirit of Truth in my friends and loved ones to guide them and direct them. The responsibility is not mine but God's. My response is my ability to recognize the Spirit of Truth that dwells in them.

And so it is.

7

SEEING THE GLORY OF GOD

---

*Dost thou know the balancing of the clouds, the won-
drous works of him which is perfect in knowledge?*
—Job 37:16

The Bible is so expressive. Take, for instance, that
wonderful passage from Isaiah which states: *The desert
shall rejoice, and blossom as the rose. It shall blossom abun-
dantly, and rejoice even with joy and singing.*[1]

Does that sound strange to you? Had you pictured
the desert as a desolate place, about as far removed
from a rose garden as you could imagine? I did. And
then, I discovered the desert in bloom, the miracle of
springtime in the desert!

Isaiah goes on to say: *And they shall see the glory of the*

---

1. Isa. 35:1, 2.

Lord, and the excellency of our God.[2] How true! Such glory I had never seen. My heart, too, rejoiced *with joy and singing.* Every little cactus, every little spiny succulent in bloom, acres and acres carpeted in pink, or yellow, or purple, stretching as far as the eye could see. Trees in bloom, huge cactus in bloom in every direction! I had never seen such flamboyant color, such dramatic effects. On one side of the road, everything was pink without a break, as far as the eye could see. On the other side, purple ground cover carpeted the sand. And then I saw the roses, the most beautiful red roses growing out of prickly cactus! What a lesson nature (God at work) has for us. Most of the year, you dare not get near these seemingly hostile plants, lest their needles pierce you. Often the desert seems hostile, though beautiful at any time; but now, in bloom, it is filled with Love, Love that envelopes you in Its glory.

It is the feeling that the soul knows after it has gone through a long, dark night when no relief seemed near. And then the Light burst through, the Presence was felt, and the parched, arid wilderness of human consciousness *blossomed as the rose.* Love walked in, in all Its glory, and the soul was no longer alone and afraid. How better could the Psalmist express it? Why would anyone want to rewrite the Bible in a literal style when it has so much feeling in its mystic poetry?

Make a special effort, if you live in California or some

2. Isa. 35:2.

other desert area, to visit the desert in the spring. And when you do, may it be for you a spiritual experience. Remember the words of Isaiah as you revel in the surge of Life bursting out on every side:

> *Then the eyes of the blind shall be opened, and the ears of the deaf shall be unstopped. Then shall the lame man leap as an hart, and the tongue of the dumb sing: for in the wilderness shall waters break out, and the streams in the desert. And the parched ground shall become a pool, and the thirsty land springs of water: in the habitation of dragons, where each lay, shall be grass with reeds and rushes. . . . And the ransomed of the Lord shall return, and come to Zion* [that high place in consciousness which the Bible calls the "Holy City"] *with songs and everlasting joy upon their heads: they shall obtain joy and gladness, and sorrow and sighing shall flee away.*[3]

It happens in the desert to remind us that it happens in the soul when we are willing to let the renewing process of Life have Its way with us. When we are willing to surrender our lives, with all of their problems; when we are willing to admit we can no longer struggle alone, then there are streams in our desert, and the wilderness within blossoms as the rose. When we let the kingdom of God rule in our lives—when we let "Thy will be done"—a great joy wells up within us; our hearts sing in exultation. Then we come to the high mountain of consciousness with joy and gladness, and sorrow and sighing flee away. When you see the desert in

3. Isa. 35:5–7, 10.

bloom, you will know what I mean, for it is like a picture of a spiritual experience.

MEDITATION

Turning away from the loneliness of despair and confusion, I let the living water of Truth flow in. Now the desolation of my mind becomes filled with the beauty of God. The desert of my lonely mind is now filled with the Presence until *it blossoms as the rose*. I am no longer alone. Anxiety fades away and my soul is filled with the wonder and glory of God because I trust in Him.

And so it is.

CHAPTER

8

THE WONDER-WORKING POWER IS ALIVE IN YOU AND ME

For it is God which worketh in you both to will and to do of his good pleasure.

—Phil. 2:13

Not long ago, I received a letter directed specifically to my attention. One of our Abundant Living readers wrote:

"You quote in one of your articles this verse from the scripture: *Draw nigh to God, and he will draw nigh to you.*[1] Now, I ask you, how in the world does one draw nigh to God?"

I do not have the letter handy, but as I remember, these were the exact words.

1. James 4:8.

How does one draw nigh to God? First, I must ask our friend, Where is God? If we think that God is up in the heavens, a very old man with a long white beard, writing our sins down in a huge ledger, it's going to be hard to get very close to Him. Where do *you* think God is?

I am reminded of a day, long ago, when I was driving along a country road with my little daughter, then age three. She looked up at me with big eyes and asked, "Mommy, where is God?"

"God is within you," I answered glibly.

"Is he in my tummock?" She wanted to know.

This took a little thought. What was I to say at that point? Did Jesus feel this challenged when they asked him when the Kingdom of God should come?

Paul felt the nearness of God when he said: *That they should seek the Lord, if haply they might feel after him, and find him though he be not far from every one of us: for in him we live and move and have our being.*[2]

How could we be any closer? Through this realization, we draw nigh unto God; we worship Him in Spirit and in Truth; we know Him in the Holy of Holies within us, for we are one with Him. There is only one life, the Life of God living through us, beating our hearts, His Life pulsing through our veins, functioning in our bodies, giving us breath moment by moment. His Wisdom guides us, teaches us, protects us if we are willing to listen and follow it. His Love is a gentle presence within us and all around us. The moment we turn to It, It is there to comfort and sustain

2. Acts 17:27, 18.

41

us. God is omnipresent, which means there is no place where He is not. How do we *draw nigh unto God?* We are there already. *And ye shall seek me, and find me, when ye shall search for me with all your heart.*[3]

God is alive! Just to say the words is inspiring. God lives in you and me. Paul called the divinity within us *Christ in you, the hope of glory.* And again, he said: *For it is God which worketh in you both to will and to do of his good pleasure.*[4] Jesus called it *the Father within; the Kingdom of God within you.*

Let this mind be in you, which was also in Christ Jesus: who, being in the form of God, thought it not robbery to be equal with God,[5] wrote Paul to the Philippians.

Whenever we are tempted to be afraid, to feel ourselves separated from the Oneness of Life, let us remember: God lives! He is there, right within us, *closer than breathing, nearer than hands and feet.* God is our life and the life around us. He will not leave us or forsake us. Fear is simply lack of trust in God; fear is doubting that God is taking care of us and our affairs. Fear, as someone has said, is faith in the enemy. Fear is believing that God is dead.

The evidence for Life divine is all around us, pulsing through our veins. Every breath proves that God is alive; God lives in us. Not only are we His children, but an extension of His own perfect Life, just as the rays

3. Jer. 29:13.
4. Phil. 2:13.
5. Phil. 2:5.

42

of the sun are a part of the sun, just as a drop of water in the ocean is a part of the deep. There is no place where God is not. If divine Life ceased for a single moment, there would be a complete void—no Intelligence, no Power, no breath of Life, no man to be aware of it All. How can we doubt that God is All in All when all the evidence supports it? GOD IS ALIVE! We live because we are ideas in the Mind of God, forever safe in His Presence.

MEDITATION

I praise the Life of God within me. It breathes through me, beats my heart, digests my food, and controls all of my bodily functions.

The Life of God within me is in harmony with all of Life. Therefore, I am in harmony with all of Life. I am guided and protected in all that I do.

And so it is.

9

I AM THE PLACE WHERE
THE LIGHT SHINES THROUGH

---

*Arise and shine; for thy light is come, and the glory
of the Lord is risen upon thee.*

—Isa. 60:1

Each one of us is a part of the perfect Life of God as
drops of water in the ocean are a part of that vast body
of water; as the microcosm (the individual) is a part of
the macrocosm (the universe).

SOMETIMES A MENTAL PICTURE HELPS

I once heard a lecturer describe it this way. He said
that he flew over a beautiful green valley in a small
plane. Looking down, he could see that there were

many springs bubbling up here and there. Wherever there was an opening, the underground body of water burst through—the same water but many individual expressions of it.

In my meditation, it came to me that another analogy might be to picture a high rock wall with open doors that let the light shine through. The sunlight is there on the other side of the wall ready to shine through wherever there is an opening. Now picture many doors and through each door the Light pouring forth making a pathway of light in front of the wall.

So it came to me, I am a door. I am the place where the Light shines through. I am a mere chink in the wall, really; but through me the Light pours forth. I am not the only door. There are many doors that let the Light shine through. Some are tall and narrow, some are wide and completely unobstructed, others are so blocked by rocks and roots that the Light is unable to penetrate them. The same Light shines through each door, bursting through every crack and crevice that will admit it. I am the door. I embody the Light as It passes through me. I am that Light in the degree that I let It come through.

The Light never stops shining. It is always so willing, ceaselessly exploring the cracks in the rock for another place to shine through.

I am only a door; and yet, through me, something wonderful is happening. As the Light shines down upon the earth at my feet, a patch of tender green appears. It is the same size and shape that I am. Here grass and flowers are able to grow. I take a certain pride in my little garden patch and yet I cannot claim it. It is the product of the Light as it meets the willing earth. It is my glory that I let the Light shine through me.

Farther on, down the wall, is a very large door. So much of the Light shines through its opening that a beautiful tree is able to bloom in its path. Would that I might borrow some of its Light so that a tree might blossom on my patch of earth. The Light that shines through me produces flowers for me. I can no more borrow from another than I can share the glory in front of me. The soil is willing. I am receptive, but the Light gives the increase. Pour through me, Light, that I may behold Thy glorious handiwork.

JESUS, THE CHRIST, UNDERSTOOD SO WELL

I am the door, spoke the Christ, accepting the Light for every son of God. Each one is a "door" admitting, in some degree, divine illumination. Through each door, the Light continues to shine. In the Light grows the fruitage of each one's experience. No matter how we long to share the Light that shines through us, our spiritual understanding cannot always be appreciated by another. Each one is given his own garden of the soul. The same Light is available to all, shining continuously.

Every good gift and every perfect gift cometh from above,

and cometh down from the Father of lights, with whom is no variableness, neither shadow of turning.[1] If you would receive Life's fruitage, chip out the rocks of doubt, uproot the weeds of despair in your "door," and let the Light shine through to everlasting glory.

Know for yourself: *I am the door. I am the way of Light. I am the place where the Light shines through.*

NOW IS THE TIME

The kingdom of God already exists. The kingdom of infinite Goodness already is. It does not need time to come into being. It already is. It is we who have taken so long to receive it.

When the Pharisees, who were always splitting hairs in an endeavor to trap Jesus, asked him when the kingdom of God should come, they thought that they had really stumped him. Certainly their lives and the lives of those of that day were no indication of the glorious kingdom of God, and who could say, they reasoned, when perfection could be attained.

But, Jesus answered them: *The kingdom of God cometh not with observation: Neither shall they say, Lo here! or, Lo there! for, behold, the kingdom of God is within you.*[2] The kingdom of God *cometh not*, for the kingdom of God is *now*. Right *now* is the divine creation perfect;

1. James 1:17.
2. Luke 17:20.

right *now* is man the image and likeness of God; right *now* is divine right action everywhere present.

"But it doesn't seem that way," you say? Try accepting the kingdom of divine perfection, the dominion of all Goodness, right *now*. You will be surprised what this will do for you. The other day, I had a realization of this, and everything started to happen at once. Several telephone calls reported progress, immediate progress, where there had seemed to be none a few minutes earlier. The salesman reported he had started selling; another said that a heavy chest cold dissolved into nothingness; a third person reported activity for real estate that seemed impossible to move. Believe me, it was thrilling. *The kingdom of God is now.*

All too often, we look forward to better conditions tomorrow. It is going to get better, we say. Tomorrow something will happen; but tomorrow is always tomorrow. Tomorrow never comes. Jesus prayed always in the present tense. The dominion of divine perfection is not *coming*, for behold the kingdom of God *is within you now.*

Say not ye, There are yet four months, and then cometh the harvest? Behold, I say unto you, Lift up your eyes, and look on the fields; for they are white already to harvest.[3] When we say, *There are yet four months*, the harvest is *always* four months away. Today is God made manifest in the only place that counts—the kingdom of God within. When we come to realize this, it seems as if time

3. John 4:35.

is speeded up for us. We telescope time, for, after all, *a thousand years are as a day in the eyes of the Lord.*[4] The perfect result already *is*, in consciousness. The Invisible already has a body the moment it is recognized, and we will see it sooner than we think if we take our anxious thought away from tomorrow; for tomorrow is always tomorrow, but the kingdom of God is *now*.

MEDITATION

There Is No Other Life

If God is All in all, there is no Life
  apart from God.
If God is the Truth of Being, nothing
  can exist apart from God.

And so it is.

4. 2 Peter 3:8.

49

10

DO WE REALLY BELIEVE WHAT WE SAY WE BELIEVE?

Trust in the Lord with all thine heart; and lean not unto thine own understanding. In all thy ways acknowledge him, and he shall direct thy paths.
—Prov. 3:5, 6

One time, I heard an evangelist give a rousing radio talk. I've never forgotten it. The theme was: "Are we walkin' what we're talkin'?"

Every now and then, I ask myself: "Do we really believe what we say we believe? And, if we do, are we willing to act on our belief?"

If we *really believed* that there *is* only One Life, *one perfect Life*, and that we are a part of that perfect Life, would we not all be healed of whatever imperfection we had *thought* belonged to us? If there *is* only One Life

and that Life is the Life of God everywhere present—
if God is all in all, omnipresent, perfect in every way—
how can there be sickness? If the Creator created us in
His image and likeness and pronounced His creation
good, how can it be less than good? The divine proto-
type would have to be imperfect for the creation to be
less than perfect. God would have to be sick for us to
be sick. How about that?

If we really believed in the One Power, all-Powerful;
if we really believed that all that the Father hath is
ours; we would have access to all-Power and be able to
say with Jesus: *All Power is given to me in heaven and in
earth.* Nothing would be too difficult. Nothing would
be impossible if we really believed in the One Power,
all-Power, omnipresent. All-Power would flow through
us and accomplish all that we needed to do.

If we really believed that God *is* Love, all-inclusive
Love everywhere present, perfect Love with us, in us,
loving us now, we could never be lonely again. Wars,
and rumors of wars, would cease. There would be no
conflict or inharmony among us, for we would all love
each other. Where is hate if Love is all there is, everywhere present?

If we really believed that God is all there is—one divine Substance, infinite, endless Abundance, everywhere present, we would no longer feel that we had to
grab and get from others, for we would know that all
that we needed was right where we are. There would
be no lack anywhere. We would dwell in the midst of
infinite resources forever available to us. Whatever we

needed we would mentally appropriate for ourselves, knowing that the loving Source would delight in pouring Itself out to us in an exuberance of every good thing.

If we really believed in the One Mind, all-knowing, all-wise, then we would know what we needed to know the moment we needed to know it. Living in a sea of Mind, the knowledge and wisdom needed would never be far from us. Like fish depending on the sea, we would depend on Mind, and the medium of Mind would constantly sustain us. If an idea was needed, we would joyously pluck it out of Mind. There would never be a moment's anxiety. Decisions? Guidance? They would be automatic. They would come from within us as needed. As the birds are guided in their journeys, we would always know the way to go.

Perhaps this is what Jesus meant when he said: *Except ye become as little children ye cannot enter into the kingdom of heaven.*[1]

If the Kingdom of Heaven is within us, depending on a childlike faith, then it is time we believed what we say we believe that we may enter into the perfect Life of God, which was prepared for us from the beginning. One perfect Life, each one a part of a perfect Whole, each one perfect and free, needing nothing, complete right where we are. *O ye of little faith!* Why do we ever doubt?

1. Matt. 18:3.

MEDITATION

I Believe

I believe that God's Perfect Life is all there is.
I believe that God's Life is omnipresent.
Therefore, It includes me and all those
   whom I would help.

And so it is.

PART II

EXPERIENCING THE WONDER-WORKING POWER

That I may publish with the voice of thanksgiving, and tell of all thy wondrous works.

—Psalm 26:7

11

OVERCOMING STRESS AND TENSION

Stand still and consider the wondrous works of God.
—Job 37:14

Today we hear a lot about stress—how to overcome stress and tension. There is a way to say goodbye to stress forever. It begins with letting the Wonder-working Power take charge of one's life.

THY WILL BE DONE

Not my will, but thine, be done. Jesus said it in the garden of Gethsemane as he faced the greatest over-coming of his life. *Father, if thou be willing, remove this cup from me: nevertheless not my will, but thine, be done.*[1] And so, we got the idea that *Thy will* meant renunciation, giving up what we really wanted and taking some great challenge, usually suffering of some sort, as the will of God. Let's take a second look at these words that Jesus thought important enough to include in the all-inclusive Lord's Prayer.

Not my will, but thine, be done. To say these words and rightly understand them is the end to every tension, limitation, and frustration—the beginning of freedom and power. To say them with complete surrender, no sense of reservation, no attempt to hold out in some small department where we know better than God, is to have achieved the mountain-moving kind of faith that takes hold and goes to work for us.

Not my will, but thine, be done. In the old days, we said it with a sigh. "All right, God, then I give up! Have it Your way and somehow I will bear it." I wonder why we thought His will meant trials for us, renunciation, long-suffering, grim endurance? Why was it that we blamed all sorts of lack and suffering, disease, and accidents on the God of Love and Peace? How could we have expected Him to will for us that which was so unlike His nature?

1. Luke 22:42.

WE CAN AFFORD TO TRUST IT

But now we know better. We know that the *will* of God must conform to the *nature* of God, something new and fresh and infinitely right for us. When we understand that the will of God is really for our highest good, we can afford to trust it. This is perhaps one of the most important revelations in our spiritual unfoldment. We remember the words of the Master, *It is your Father's good pleasure to give you the kingdom.*[2] The kingdom is spiritual dominion. No suffering or denial there.

Not my will, but thine, be done. We say it now with a sigh of contentment. Like a tired child who goes to sleep secure in mother's arms, we can relax. No longer must we struggle to make something happen. And now something *does* happen.

Whoever said I had to follow a profession I did not like? Surround myself with unhappy people? Live in an unsuitable environment? God's will for me is done easily, harmoniously, and joyously, and I am now free to realize the desires of my heart. It seems like magic. I meet the right people, the right doors are opened so effortlessly for me. My demonstration is here. It came while I wasn't looking. It all started the day I said *Thy will be done* and meant it.

What do we mean when we pray: *Thy will be done?* When I pray *Thy will be done*, I mean that I am agreeing with the perfect will of God for me. I am letting go

2. Luke 12:32.

of my human will and letting the divine will be done in and through my life.

What is the perfect will of God for me? It is all that God is! Therefore, I am letting go and letting God infuse my spirit. I am letting go and letting God have full course in my life. In letting the will of God be done, I am letting divine Right Action be the law of my life. I am letting the Peace of God that passes all understanding fill my mind, as I pray: *Let thy will be done.*

Letting the will of God rule is letting the Love of God fill my heart to overflowing, letting infinite Love shelter me and my world.

Letting the perfect will of God come in includes inspiration, all the ideas I can use, ideas that well up within me and spill over into every area of my livingness.

The will of God for me is abundance, an abundance of every good thing. It flows through my affairs with such lavishness that there is not room enough to receive it.

The will of God is health and vitality, strength and serenity. It is all this and a thousand times more. It is Power to move mountains; Beauty and Joy beyond my dreams. It is Wisdom and Justice that adjusts every difficulty with fairness, hurting no one.

IT'S THE HIGHEST FORM OF PRAYER

Let thy will be done is the highest form of prayer, all-inclusive. It cleanses the mind of all imperfection so that we can no longer remember the pending problems. *Let thy will be done* is all that we need, in one beautiful package. It wraps it all up. It takes care of everything.

Let thy will be done is agreement with that perfect Life that knows no deviation from Itself. Once Thy kingdom has been established in us, we can trust that Life to include our life: as in Thy heaven, Father, let Thy will be done in my earth! It is precisely when we are able to trust completely in that Life which is without mistake that we see that Joseph was right: "they" may have *meant it for evil but God meant it unto good!*[3] Nothing can possibly hurt us when we trust the will of God for us. All things *do* work together for good.

Thy will be done. Except the Lord build the house, they labor in vain that build it.[4] And so I ask myself, "Why am I struggling against time, battling with the confusions of the day?" *For what is a man profited, if he shall gain the whole world, and lose his own soul?*[5] It would be better to sit down for five minutes and contemplate Thy will for me. I do. Peace fills my heart. I am able to say with St. Augustine: *Lord, walk these feet.* God lives

3. Gen. 50:20.
4. Ps. 127:1.
5. Matt. 16:26.

through me, and no responsibility rests with me except to love Him with all my heart and soul and mind, to trust Him completely. Gone is the pressure of the day that was sapping my energy. With new creative inspiration, I tackle the job at hand. Each step falls into place. A telephone call cancels out one bothersome job that had troubled me. There are some things I find I can delegate to others. Somehow the deadline that frustrated me has been miraculously extended. Before the day is over, my desk is clear and I am free. Never can I doubt Thy will again!

Thy will be done! We come to sing it as a psalm of praise and thanksgiving. There is a perfect plan for each of us! It is His will for us to live fully and joyously. Sickness and suffering, loneliness and limitation, were never His way. Yes, surely, *eye hath not seen, nor ear heard, neither have entered into the heart of man, the things which God hath prepared for them that love him.*[6]

> *My will in thee is joy not sorrow,*
> *My will in thee is faith not fear,*
> *My will in thee is awareness of*
>   *my love for thee,*
> *Let my will within thee be done.*

—Upanishads

6. 1 Cor. 2:9.

12

THE EASY WAY AND
THE HARD WAY

*. . . that ye might be filled with the knowledge of his
will in all wisdom and spiritual understanding.*
—Col. 1:9

In this world in which we live there are two approaches to living—an easy way and a hard way. The easy way is God's way. The hard way is the human way. There is a way of health and wholeness to which sickness and suffering are completely unknown and a way of constant suffering in which one seems to be subject to one malady after another. The healthy way is God's way. The way of imperfection is the human way. There is a life of abundance, enough and to spare, the needs met even before they appear—and there is a way of lack, of never having enough for daily needs. The way of abundance is God's way, the way of ease and plenty prepared for the children of God before the beginning of time. The way of lack is man's distortion. There is a way of ease completely free of struggle, a timeless flowing way where things fall into place without effort, almost as if by magic, an easy, happy way to live. This is God's way. This is the art of letting go and letting God.

Why is it so hard for us to let go and let God? It must be because we do not really believe that God can be trusted to take care of us and our earthly affairs.

RESENTMENT PRODUCES THISTLES

I know a man who planted a lawn. Not very unusual, you say? This one was. To begin with, it was a huge lawn covering nearly an acre on a side hill. The man was advised, because of the steep site, that seeding the ground was impossible and so he went to enormous expense to have it sodded. Truck after truck of sod was ordered. It came rolled up like a green carpet. Finally, after much grading and rolling of the soil, the sod was rolled down and fitted like carpet and there was "instant lawn."

Now the "fun" began. The man was told that he must water the sod constantly lest in the extremely hot, dry climate it dry out, in which case the beautiful "instant lawn" would turn brown and die. The man had not had a sprinkling system installed and this meant that he must stand out in the hot sun or work late at night and water this huge lawn by hand. He became furious at the thought. It was an up-hill battle from then on. He watered the new lawn, but with every drop that hit the soil, he fumed and fought. He poured not only water but fury into that lawn.

After about three days and nights of this, a strange thing happened. From somewhere, no one ever knew from where, a herd of cows got loose from some farm, quite a distance away, and somehow or other they managed to find this man's yard. In the middle of the night, while he slept, they walked all over his lawn. Up and down the hill they went, pushing the little rolls of green carpet-like sod in every direction. And, because the ground was soggy with much watering, the cows sank deep down into the ground, making hillocks and holes a foot or so deep, literally burying the sod in the mud. Around and around that house they went until there wasn't a smooth place they missed.

When the man woke up the next morning, he was madder than ever. Now he really cussed. He fought through the endless job of leveling out that sod. He had to order several loads of black dirt and lift the sod and fill the holes. It was an extra week's work, and more and more fury went into the job. Finally, it was almost the way it had been in the first place, and the watering began again. The grass began to grow. But now another strange thing happened. Russian thistles began to pop up everywhere. They looked like very spiny, prickly cactus, and they grew almost overnight to be a foot or two tall, covering the entire lawn. Each one had to be carefully dug out with a knife; and as fast as one thistle was done away with, three more came in its place. It never was a very good lawn, that lawn that was nurtured with hate—a true story, and a sad one.

THE MAN WITH A GREEN THUMB

I know another man who takes the easy way. Everything he does, he does with love. When he needed a lawn planted, his friends got together and had a lawn-planting bee; amid much fun and laughter they did it for him. This man trusted God to guide him in all that he did, and everything fell into place in a most surprising way. His friends tease him about having a green thumb, but he knows that this really means that God does the gardening for him. He, too, had a large yard. Somehow or other he happened to meet a landscape architect at a friend's house who took an interest and made a landscape plan that evening. Then the crowd got together and helped it materialize. It grew so beautifully. There were no weeds in this man's garden and, believe it or not, it rained just at the time the new plants needed the most water.

As Paul remarked, *I have planted, Apollos watered, but God gave the increase.*[1] It is easy to see here which man

1. 1 Cor. 3:6.

66

followed God's way, the easy way. The art is letting go and letting God do it.

When we get ourselves out of the way, everything flows. It doesn't matter whether it is health, or wealth, or garden-planting. It all begins with a relaxed mind that lets God's perfect Life flow through into perfect manifestation.

CONTRAST THESE TWO BUSINESS PEOPLE

Now, therefore, thus sayeth the Lord of hosts; Consider your ways. Ye have sown much, and bring in little; ye eat, but ye have not enough: ye drink, but ye are not filled with drink; ye clothe you, but there is none warm; and he that earneth wages, earneth wages to put it into a bag with holes.[2]

I know a woman who had a real challenge in her work. She was a top executive in the company for which she worked. She was a veritable genius, and the success of the company was really due, in large measure, to her ability and talent. She was a designer, and her designs sold like hotcakes, but she was taken for granted by the management. She was underpaid, overworked, and unappreciated. She had every right to be mad, and mad she was. She fussed and fumed and raged until her creativeness was thoroughly impaired.

2. Hag. 1:5,6.

Finally, she resigned and was unable to find another position. Her life was wasted. The potential was there, but she failed to let go and let God.

Contrast this experience with a man I know who had just as much reason to contend with the company for which he worked. He, too, seemed to be unappreciated and to go unrewarded for his ability and productiveness. He, too, was tempted to contend with the situation. Being a Truth student, he refused to succumb to the temptation. He said, "I will not contend with this, I will release this problem to the infinite Intelligence within me. God has a perfect plan for me, and it will be revealed at the right and perfect time." He went on giving his best and trusting the perfect Power of God within him.

God did have a wonderful plan for him. A terrific idea was given to him. It came easily and was worked out for him, through him, as if by magic. He was given a patent on his idea. Now everyone wants the product, something for which there had long been a need. I wouldn't be surprised if he became a millionaire through this divine idea that was handed to him because he released his problem and trusted. He let go and let God. He took the creative way, which is God's way.

Except the Lord build the house, they labor in vain that build it: except the Lord keep the city, the watchman waketh but in vain.[3]

3. Ps. 127:1.

In the symbolic language of the Bible, this simply means that unless we demonstrate our good through the orderly process of planting the idea in mind and letting go and letting God produce the manifestation in the right and perfect way, we struggle and strive with those results—that is, we *labor in vain*.

The Bible also tells us, *A man can receive nothing, except it be given him from heaven*,[4] which is to say that unless the idea is first planted in mind (the Bible calls it the heaven within), it cannot be received in the outer manifestation.

This does not mean that we are to fold our hands and sit under a tree. Far from it. God works for us, through us. We must take the necessary footsteps. Mentally we must let go. No fretting and fuming, nor rat-race thinking and stewing, nor worry and anxiety. Then, and only then, can the Father within do the work. There is an old saying of the East: "To the man who can most perfectly practice inaction, all things are possible." Not physical inaction, but inaction of the little human mind that spends itself on useless worry.

In his book *Let Go and Let God*, the late Albert Cliffe tells the story of the two little frogs that fell into a pail of thick cream. One frog was filled with fear and panicked. Around and around he swam. Finally he became exhausted, was choked by the cream, and died. Not so the other frog. He knew that he was going to get out of that pail somehow, and he said to himself as he looked over his shoulder at the drowning frog,

4. John 3:27.

"That isn't going to happen to me!" Because he affirmed his good and did not panic, he received from his heaven within a beautiful idea that saved his life. He placed his front feet against the pail and started to paddle for all he was worth with his back feet. In no time he had a pat of butter. With this solid island beneath his feet, he hopped out.

Which frog let go and let God? Surely not the one that got into a panic and swam around in circles. No, the one that did the good job of paddling with his feet must have mentally released his problem long enough to receive the good inspiration that saved his life. There is always an idea that will get us out of any difficulty if we will just be still long enough to hear it and then act upon it.

All Power belongeth unto God, said the Psalmist, and Jesus said, *All Power is given unto me in heaven [within] and in earth [the outer]*. Once we have received the divine Inspiration, the Lord builds the house for us and everything falls into place in an orderly fashion. This is the easy way, but oh! how we waste ourselves huffing and puffing in a futile effort to manhandle the problem all by ourselves! It's just that we sometimes forget that there is an easy way and, perhaps, many of us do not know how to let go and let God.

THE CONSCIENTIOUS TYPE

It is easier for the easygoing type of person to let go and let God. If you can be a little bit lazy and not let unfinished business bother you, if you can take a lazy, lying-in-the-sun attitude, accomplishing little by little whatever you can, you are so much better off. It is the person who has been brought up from a child to do the best he can, to feel that everything depends upon his efforts, the hard-hitting, hard-driving, overly conscientious type that needs to pay special attention to the art of letting go and letting God. Carrying the world on your shoulders will only cause back trouble.

FOR THE ONE WHO IS BOTHERED BY OVERLOAD

If you feel that you are continually burdened, that there is just too much to do, try this approach: Stand back a bit and say to yourself: "Suppose I don't get all of these books written; suppose the yard doesn't get cultivated this week, this month, or this year; is the world going to come to an end? Will anyone know it a hundred years from now?" Tell yourself, "I'll just do one thing at a time, patiently plugging away, satisfied with what the Lord accomplishes through me." This seems to release a fresh spurt of energy.

Next, say: "All right, Father, what do you want me to do next? What would you like to do through me? I will take one step at a time. Use these hands, Lord, walk these feet." As the song says, "Take my life and let it be consecrated, Lord, to Thee." Such a light feeling comes over you. Everything falls into place. The work that you do gets done easily and in half the time. This is letting go and letting God.

DON'T LET THOSE CHALLENGES FRIGHTEN YOU

Sometimes the challenges we face get all out of proportion. Like the little girl who told her mother that she had seen a great big lion in the park. Of course, her mother didn't believe her, but the little girl insisted that she had seen a lion in the park. That night, the mother said to the little girl as she was ready to hear her prayer, "When you say your prayers, dear, ask God to forgive you for telling that falsehood about the lion in the park." The little girl said her prayers and then she was silent for a long time, her eyes tightly closed. Finally, she opened her eyes with a big smile. "And did you ask God to forgive you?" the mother asked. "Yes," said the little girl, "and do you know what He said? He said, 'Never mind, dear, I've often been fooled by that big dog myself!'"

No matter how scary your problem may be, it is just trying to be a lion in your life. It has no power because there is only Power in God, infinite Good, right where you are.

RELEASING THROUGH THANKSGIVING

One very helpful way to release one's problems is to start out by giving thanks. Usually we find that we have become so engrossed in the problem at hand that we are looking at the hole instead of the doughnut. At such times, it is beneficial to make a list of all of the things for which we can give thanks. When I do this, I find that I have received many answers. The things that I asked for yesterday and last week and last month have been arriving steadily and faithfully, and all of the time I was so busy looking at the needs ahead that I had failed to give God credit for the good received. I then feel like a most ungrateful wretch and see that I don't need to get into a stew about this new need, that I can afford to let go and let God. I see that God has been faithful to His promise all along the line.

LETTING GO AND LETTING GOD
IN A CRISIS

There are times in our lives when we are faced with a crisis. At such times, the world seems to descend upon us and we find ourselves sinking in the quicksand of self-pity and disappointment. What would be a crisis in your life may not be a crisis in my life; the challenging situation in my life may not bother you at all. It all depends upon what we hold most dear. If something is overly important to us, then the loss of it is going to be especially difficult. What is your treasure? Then beware, for you must be prepared to release it, if necessary, without a backward look.

Suppose someone steals your wife. Suppose your child is in an accident. Suppose the market drops as in the famous crash of 1929 and you are suddenly left penniless. How are you going to meet the crisis?

Let's take a case that we have all heard or read about: your house or business burns and with it many personal items that can never be replaced—your favorite books, your favorite pictures, valuable papers, sentimental items, etc. You discover that it was an act of arson and you feel terribly hurt to think that someone was so unloving as to deliberately try to destroy you and these things that meant so much to you. It isn't just the value, but it now seems hard to feel God's love. What are you going to do about it?

Two roads stretch before you. The choice is yours. Which way will you go? As with every crisis, one road leads to death and destruction. You can become bitter, you can rail at life. You can tell your sad story over and over to every new listener. You can lie awake nights in an endless merry-go-round of futile thinking, picturing again and again that awful moment when you first came upon the desolation and ruin that had been presented to you. You can make yourself ill and even take yourself out of this world through this approach. Certainly you will make yourself unpopular—and where will it get you? Absolutely nowhere, except a hell on earth of your own making.

The other road is really the easy way. It is the way of letting go and letting God. It takes self-discipline, but it can be done, and the rewards are many. It takes releasing of all personal possessions, even the things of intangible value. It takes blessing the entire situation for good, not once, but over and over again. It means blessing the person who seems to have been an enemy. It means surrendering the entire situation. This is the glorious road to victory. The greater the crisis, the greater the reward, until the good never stops coming back to bless you. *I will restore to you the years that the locust hath eaten.*[5] In the end, you will find that the person whose act seemed to bring you suffering was really your benefactor, that you are not a victim, but one blessed. *Anything that makes us reach spiritually, anything that causes us to completely surrender our lives to God,* opens the door to spiritual riches untold. The bigger the problem, the more staggering the crisis, the richer the spiritual reward will be. *The battle is not yours but the Lord's.* When you let the Lord meet it for you, you will find, as did the army of Jehoshaphat, that once the enemy thought/people have been overcome, you are three days gathering up the precious jewels. The spiritual growth is so great, you can never explain it to another. Best of all, this particular experience can never terrify you again. You have faced it. You have met it and the victory is yours.

5. Joel 2:25.

LETTING GO AND LETTING GOD PLEASE OTHERS

One of the things that cause us to get tense and jumpy is trying to please other people. Sometimes it gets to be a regular fetish with us. We try to please parents; we try to please the teacher, the boss, the wife or husband; and the harder we try, the harder they are to please. Actually, our efforts seem to work against us. It's a funny thing about human nature: There is a little tyrant in us all, and, when we find that someone is standing on his head trying to please, we rather enjoy making him squirm. Some people take positive pride in *not* being pleased. The truth is that we can never please personality. Personality is human and unpredictable. The answer is to please God and let people go. Then you please everybody. As long as we continue to try to please people, we are going to be disappointed in people, hurt by people. Let go and let God in *you* please God in *them*. It is the only way to win this battle.

Say to yourself, "The Christ in me salutes the Christ in you. God in you knows what to do. I release you to your own God expression. I let go and let God in you guide and direct you. I trust God in you to respond to God in me and maintain peace and harmony between us. Since God is all there is, we are one, one perfect Life expressed in many ways."

SURRENDER YOUR PROBLEMS TO GOD

God is able. We can trust God. We can *let go and let God* without a moment's fear. *Nothing is impossible to God.*

God is able to make all grace abound toward you: that ye, always having all sufficiency in all things, may abound to every good work.[6]

6. 2 Cor. 9:8.

CHAPTER

13

FINDING TRUE HAPPINESS
---

*Happy is the man that findeth wisdom, and the man
that getteth understanding.*

—Prov. 3:13

When we have learned, at least in a measure, to keep
the world in its proper place—under our feet—we are
able to look about us with a feeling of detachment. We
know that as far as material goals are concerned, we
can have anything that we desire if we go about it right.
When this realization comes, somehow the thing that
we once thought so important takes a secondary place.
The old striving, born of frustration, has gone out of
our desires. We are like children, who, having been told
that they can have all of the candy they want, no
longer grab for the nearest piece but become discriminating in their selection. All of a sudden, we have

a new set of values. I agree with Krishnamurti, who told his students:

> *When you do have some measure of detachment, however little, you enjoy life much more. The things that we experience are as garments for our adornment that we put on or take off without being identified with them.*

AN UNDERSTANDING OF IMPERSONAL LOVE

The next step is an understanding of impersonal love. Eventually, we come to the place in our spiritual growth where we can be alone or in the midst of a crowd without being lonely. We enjoy human love and friendship, but we do not have to have people to feed upon emotionally. Wherever we are, we are already immersed in a sea of divine Love, and the love that we receive from others is but the reflection of the Love we have already received within.

Those who have experienced these two steps in their spiritual unfoldment are now ready to devote their lives to helping others in their search for Truth. In the measure of their own growth, they draw others to them who seek the treasure that they have to share.

Now a very interesting thing happens. The one who has done the overcoming along a certain line is now confronted with the very same problem all over again—but this time it is in the second dimension. He sees the same struggle for freedom going on in the life of someone else. This time he is the bystander, interested but not emotionally caught up in the problem. He views the struggle with compassion but, at the same time, with detachment. Having already overcome a similar challenge, he is able to hold out a lifeline to his brother. Having found the Omnipresence in his own situation, he knows that once again the battle is the Lord's. This time, the conquest is easier because he knows that the victory, having been established, is now assured, and he is also able to see his friend's problem in a detached manner. He is not emotionally embroiled in it. This is the role of the minister or practitioner. This is why it is advisable to seek spiritual help when we have become too close to a problem ourselves.

There are, however, those who are able to develop this inner security for themselves. Some are able to step aside and view the problem in their own lives with the same feeling of detachment that they would have if they were viewing a play upon a stage. As one of my friends remarked the other day, "To be successful in this drama of life, we need to stop trying to be the Director and be willing to be an actor!" And, quick as a wink, another person added, "I've found it's best to stop trying to be the author, too!"

The illumined all agree. Happiness comes only to those who are willing to surrender their lives to the divine Author, the divine Director, and finally to watch the divine Self act out the play the way it ought to be acted. This is another way of saying, *he who loses his life shall find it*, or *that which we give away, we keep*. To be the onlooker is to have learned true detachment.

MEDITATION

I Am Subject Only to God

What is that to thee? Follow thou me.
—John 21:26

Man lives by divine decree. There is a law of divine Harmony that brings our lives into balance as we turn to it.

I know that God's Law is operating in my life and affairs right now. God has a plan for me, and His Love goes before me and prepares the way for each step in its unfoldment.

I do not have to explain or apologize for any action I may have taken in the past. I do not have to justify my actions of the present or have man's approval of my future actions. God and I are a majority. I turn to God for my directions. I do not depend upon man or man's opinion of me. I listen only to the still, small voice within me that tells me, moment by moment, what I should do. God has a perfect plan for me, and, as I wait trustingly, it is revealed to me at just the right time.

I cease to try to please my friends and relatives.

Only the Spirit within me knows what is truly right for me. As I follow my inner Guidance, I feel relaxed and free.

I know that I am in the right place, doing the right thing at the right time. Each situation is an opportunity to learn more of God's Truth and glorify God right where I am. As I know this, all fear is taken out of the situation and the way is made clear. What was right for me yesterday may not be right for me today. What is right for me today will undoubtedly need to be changed and expanded tomorrow. I am completely flexible. I rejoice that infinite Intelligence is able to look ahead for my tomorrows. I trust the perfect plan God has for me.

I am dedicated to God's Truth. I respond only to God's authority. I depend upon God's loving care for me. Divine Love leads me and cares for me each step of the way.

And so it is.

CHAPTER

14

LITTLE MIRACLES THAT
CHANGE OUR LIVES

---

*Unto thee, O God, do we give thanks, unto thee do
we give thanks: for that thy name is near thy wondrous works declare.*

—Ps. 75:1

To some it is given to experience dramatic miracles
of healing. I have seen life restored instantaneously at
what has been called "the eleventh hour." Periodically,
we are privileged to share in these dramatic healings
and there is a glow that lingers on from them, enlarg-
ing our faith for many days to come.

But, there are little miracles that change our lives
from day to day. In them, we see the fine hand of God
at work. It is in little ways that our lives are trans-
formed and we receive the necessary proof of the

Wonder-working Power in action, so needed to keep us on the upward path.

A SERIES OF LITTLE MIRACLES

A friend of mine, a retired lady, was lonely. She lived in a house with several other women, but they were negative, gloomy people with whom she had nothing in common. It seemed as if she were trapped in an environment from which she could not escape. Her neighbors had no use for what they called her "Pollyanna thinking" and seemed to go out of their way to convince her of the validity of sickness. Their conversations were inclined to be "organ recitals," talk about operations and the ills of the world. My friend longed for someone with whom she could talk her own affirmative language, some friend with whom she could laugh and joke and be happy. As she had no transportation, she was pretty much confined to her home. It would have to be someone who could come to her. It was not possible for her to get to church or other activities where she could meet people. She had begun to feel that it was impossible for her to meet anyone with whom she could be happy.

Then one day I felt compelled to write to her, suggesting that she open her mind to receive a "little miracle." Let's agree, I suggested, that it is possible for someone to come to you, someone you would enjoy knowing, someone with whom you can be happy and free. We agreed that it was possible for her to have the kind of companionship she craved; that someone would be drawn right to her door. Someone was. As I recall, she was a census-taker, this interesting, alive person who called on my friend. They soon discovered that they had much in common. This was the beginning of several enjoyable chats. Here was one of those "fun" miracles—the kind that happen so easily and effortlessly that we have to pinch ourselves to believe it. It was the beginning of a series of little miracles, as you shall see.

I wrote to her: "This is just the beginning. I see new friends seeking you out in ways we cannot imagine now. God has ways we know not of."

In the past, there had been years and years of loneliness, years in which it had seemed as if there were no way for her to make new friends. But now, only a few weeks later, I received another report from her. I'm sure she wouldn't mind my sharing a part of it with you, since demonstrations of this kind build the faith of all of us. She wrote me:

> "Now, for something that will amuse you. You remember telling me that you were putting in mind a request that I would be surrounded by people with whom I could chat and be happy? Well, this is what happened. Recently, I went to the hospital for a minor operation. I had hoped for a semiprivate room, but all they had for me was a room with four beds. There I

found the happy, interesting people we asked for. It was a delightful experience. Never have I been so surrounded with love. I loved the patients and the wonderful nurses, and they loved me!"

But this was only the beginning. Now we have a still more recent report:

"You remember some time ago I wrote to you telling you about some of my neighbors? I told you how kind and thoughtful they were but that they kept pouring out a deluge of negative thinking to me. The result was that we had very little in common. You wrote that you were putting a seed in mind for proper companionship for me, for fun and happy times. This is just a little note to tell you that you planted well. The two worst offenders moved away and two other women moved in. One of them is just a joy to me. She and I enjoy the same books and love the same poetry and can discuss all subjects impersonally. I just wanted you to know this."

I am humbly grateful to have been an instrument in planting new seeds for a new experience for this precious friend. It takes such a little turning in the direction of the Father's house to have the Father come out to meet us. As Jesus said, *And all things whatsoever ye shall ask in prayer, believing, ye shall receive.*[1] We asked the Father for friends, and friends came. Where loneliness had been accepted as unavoidable for many

1. Matt. 21:22.

years, now there was pleasant companionship. *Behold I make all things new!*[2] That which was imperfect had faded away. *The Lord will perfect that which concerneth me.*[3] It may seem like a little miracle, but it was mighty important to a little lady who had grown tired of living alone.

THIS ONE CAME FAST

The other day one of our volunteers came to work with an idea. "If I just had a car," she said, "I could come in and help more often. I've been thinking, maybe I could pick up an old car that would do to get me back and forth." And then she said, "Pray for me to find the right car and I'll be glad to come in more often."

"There is a perfect, right automobile for you," we told her, "one that is right for you in every way." And then, jokingly, someone added, "Remember the little old ladies in tennis shoes who have cars in the garage that they never use; maybe someone will give you a car that's not being used!"

You'll hardly believe it, but that is exactly what happened! A woman whose husband was in the hospital decided a day or two later that, as she had two cars, and one of them she didn't use at all, it would be a

2. Rev. 21:5.
3. Ps. 138:8.

good idea to let a friend use one of them. And so she telephoned our volunteer and offered it to her. "You might just as well be using it," she said, "and then, if I need you to take me to the hospital, you will have the car."

"Wondrous are the workings of the Lord," I always say. Some answers come so fast they astound us. Usually it's the little things, the things we accept without straining at life, that come into our lives easily and joyously. "Here's another little miracle!" we say. But let's not underrate them; they are harbingers of great good—for what happens in the little things is proof that the Wonder-working Power is at work in our lives and can just as easily produce great miracles, impressive miracles for all the world to see and for which to glorify the Father.

THE INSPIRATION OF THE ALMIGHTY

Not long after this, I was awakened one night with the following words being spoken in my mind—as if I heard a voice speaking to me personally, whereupon I was wide awake:

But as it is written, Eye hath not seen, nor ear heard, neither have entered into the heart of man, the things which God hath prepared for them that love him.[4]

4. 1 Cor. 2:9.

I quickly turned to the second chapter of 1 Corinthians to see what followed. It was interesting to note that Paul was quoting here from Isaiah, and he continued with this idea:

> But God hath revealed them unto us by his Spirit: for the Spirit searcheth all things, yea, the deep things of God.
>
> For what man knoweth the things of a man, save the spirit of man which is in him? Even so the things of God knoweth no man, but the Spirit of God.
>
> Now we have received, not the spirit of the world, but the spirit which is of God; that we might know the things that are freely given to us of God.[5]

These beautiful words go hand in hand with Elihu's admonition to Job:

> But there is a spirit in man: and the inspiration of the Almighty giveth them understanding.[6]

Your "little miracle" may not seem very important to someone else. The promise that unfolds to him may not be of passing interest to you. But *the inspiration of the Almighty giveth them understanding.* There is a voice that speaks to us, often *in a dream, in a vision of the night, in slumberings upon the bed.*[7] Then we know that God has not forsaken us, that even in the little things, His hand shall lead us and His right hand shall hold us safely all the days of our lives.

5. 1 Cor. 2:10–12.
6. Job 32:8.
7. Job 33:15.

CHAPTER

15

ARE YOU TOO BUSY?

Many, O Lord my God, are thy wonderful works which thou hast done . . . they cannot be reckoned up in order unto thee: if I would declare and speak of them, they are more than can be numbered.

—Ps. 40:5

Are you too busy? Are you too busy to enjoy life, too busy to relax, too busy to pray, and almost too busy to live? Do you feel sometimes as if you were spinning around on the outside of a large wheel, now and then getting tangled up with the spokes but never able to stop and rest at the center where there is peace and no motion at all?

Some years ago, I saw a wonderful cartoon in a newspaper. I wish I had kept it and could reproduce it here on this page. It was, alas! a rather good picture of most of us who hurry and hurry and never quite get there. It showed a giant clock. Its victims, chained to the hands, hurried around the outer edge, heads down, shoulders bent, with anxious, harried expressions on their faces. The caption under one little man read, "I must hurry and get there so that I can hurry and get back"; another was, "I must hurry and take my ulcer pills."

If you think that an exaggerated concept, catch a glimpse of yourself, unaware, as you hurry along the street and chance to be mirrored in a store window. I have, and I've been shocked.

"Hurry is worry and worry is fear; fear is fever and fever is death," wrote the late W. Frederic Keeler in his wonderful book *Christian Victory Instruction*. We can add to that: hurry and worry give us no time to commune with God; and when we do not take time to commune, we all but cease to live. Without the Peace of God, our lives become a futile sequence, a giant squirrel cage of frustration and despair.

SHOULD MARY HELP MARTHA?

Years ago, I remember, a woman telephoned me. "You're the wife of the minister," she said in a high, tense voice, "Your husband tells us we should 'pray without ceasing.' Now, you tell me how I'm going to do that with a baby to feed and care for, two other small children, a part-time job, a sick mother. . . . " Her voice trailed on, and I felt exhausted; it made me tired to think of it. I knew just how she felt. It reminded me of the story of Mary and Martha in the gospel of Luke.

Mary and Martha had been warring in me too, of late, and I'll admit I had been siding with Martha. It didn't seem fair that I must constantly busy myself with the endless household chores that always seemed to keep me from worshipping at the feet of the Master. And then one day I took another look at Mary and Martha, and because of what I saw, I was able to help myself and, upon this occasion, give of my growth to somebody else. Surely this dear soul had been led to call me today. *Freely ye have received, freely give.* A week before, I would have drowned with her in tears of self-pity. Today I could offer her a gift from the Spirit within, born out of the pain of my own frustration. I had worked out a way for Mary to help Martha in my own life.

Mary and Martha were the sisters of Lazarus, all good friends of Jesus. I gather that Jesus was invited there to dinner rather often. Luke tells us that Mary *sat at Jesus' feet, and heard his word.* This left Martha to do all the work and she didn't like it a bit. *Martha*, we are told, *was cumbered* (that means burdened) *about much serving.*[1] How like most of us today, burdened about much serving!

Finally, Martha complained to Jesus, just as we all complain now and then. Can't you hear her? Her voice is filled with righteous indignation, for she is expecting

1. Luke 10:38–40.

Jesus to get after Mary for not doing her part. There stands Martha, hands on hips, waiting for Jesus to say, "Now, Mary, you pitch in and help your sister! Can't you see how tired and distraught she is? Some other day we'll listen to the Word of God."

But Jesus didn't say that. He surprised Martha and probably left her speechless when he said, *Martha, Martha, thou art careful and troubled about many things: But one thing is needful; and Mary hath chosen that good part, which shall not be taken away from her.*[2]

For generations these words have rankled in the minds of hardworking, conscientious Christian women who could accept everything else in the Bible verbatim but not this seeming injustice to Martha. "After all," they said, "*somebody* had to get the dinner. We need Marthas, too!"

HOW DO MARY AND MARTHA RELATE TO US?

Who are Mary and Martha? How do they relate to us? St. Teresa said, "To give our Lord a perfect hospitality, Mary and Martha must combine." We can paraphrase this: "In order to find a perfect balance, the Mary and Martha within each one of us must unite."

Mary and Martha are phases of our own consciousness. Mary is the idealist, the philosopher, the student

2. Luke 10:41,42.

and dreamer. She seeks to know the Truth. She listens for the Christ to speak to her as inner Guidance. The Mary side of each one of us lives in the thought world; and that is good. Martha is the practical or objective side, following through with the practical human footsteps that must be taken. The action on the physical plane takes place through Martha. She receives the word of instruction from the Mary or subjective part of the mind and acts upon it in the world of affairs. *But be ye doers of the word, and not hearers only, deceiving your own selves.*[3] Martha's role is very important. The only time she gets into trouble is when she forgets *that good part* and fails to listen for the word of God before she acts. The secret is to combine Mary and Martha for a well-balanced personality.

HOW MARY HELPS MARTHA

As a means to this end, I worked out a series of "pray as you go" affirmations to be used while doing the routine chores. While these were mostly designed for the household Marthas, the idea could easily be adapted to masculine duties as well. It is hoped that they will suggest to each one an original line of contemplative thinking to fit the situation at hand.

The key idea is: "I do my work for the glory of God. As I bless my work, it blesses me. As I sit at the

3. James 1:22.

94

Master's feet with Mary, Martha's work is done easily and joyously in half the time."

THE PRACTICE OF THE PRESENCE OF GOD

A seventeenth-century monk, Brother Lawrence, was the inspiration for my "pray as you go" affirmations. One day while feeling particularly "cumbered" about my own "much serving," I was hurriedly peeling a carrot as I hurriedly prepared the stew for a hurried dinner. In my frenzy, I cut my finger. Out of that seeming evil came great good, for when I stopped a moment I thought of Brother Lawrence. Somewhere I had read that Brother Lawrence peeled even the lowly carrot for the glory of God. The idea must have made a groove in my mind, for peeling carrots, Brother Lawrence, and the "Practice of the Presence of God" went together in my mind.

"You wouldn't have cut your finger," I told myself, "if you'd been practicing the Presence." Brother Lawrence believed in praying without ceasing. He talked to God as he worked. He was able to practice the Presence among the pots and pans. He said:

> With me, my time of labour is no longer different from the time of prayer. Amid the clatter and confusion of my kitchen, when numerous people are calling various orders, I hold to God and with as great

tranquility as though I were on my knees at the blessed sacrament. . . . In His service I turn the cake that is on the pan before me. When that service is done, I kneel down in submission to Him, for it is through His grace that I have work to do. Then I rise happier than a king. For me it is enough that I but pick up a straw from the ground for the love of Him. . . .

At the beginning of my work I would speak to God with a child's faith: "O God, Thou art with me and it is Thy will that these outward tasks are given me to do; therefore I ask Thee, assist me, and through it all let me continue in Thy Presence. Be with me in this my endeavour, accept the labour of my hands, fill my heart as always."

The Practice of the Presence of God
—Brother Lawrence

Brother Lawrence had found the *one thing needful, that good part*. Brother Lawrence had found a way to worship at the feet of the Master with Mary while doing the work of Martha. The *Practice of the Presence* was the key! In his own words, he tells us that it made him "jubilant," "continuously happy," and "filled with joy so great I can hardly contain it." If Brother Lawrence could do it, why couldn't we all find a way of combining Mary and Martha to achieve peace and joy in the midst of confusion?

BRINGING GOD INTO EACH TASK

From that time on, I began to work out a system of bringing God into each task. The result was more wonderful than I could have imagined. To begin with, all sense of pressure miraculously left me and the heavy burden of things "left undone that should have been done" slipped away. To my great surprise, I began to enjoy the housework. No longer was it a waste of time. It became a game during which each moment was radiant with the Presence of God.

Even the task of bed-making made me, like Brother Lawrence, positively "jubilant." As I made each bed, I thought, "I make this bed for the glory of God. I smooth it lovingly and leave it unruffled and harmoniously perfect. I bless this bed for relaxed and perfect sleep—God's gift to me tonight. I bless the occupant of this bed and see him as the relaxed, poised Son of God he is." Somehow or other, this took all of the resistance out of bed-making. I fairly flew to the dishes, not the least bit tired after making the beds.

As I washed the dishes, I continued to talk to God. I thought, "I dedicate the time I spend washing these dishes to the worship of God. I think of the clear water flowing over the dishes as a symbol of Pure Spiritual Consciousness. With it, I wash away unnecessary substances as I let unnecessary, cluttered thoughts slip away from my mind. I leave not only the dishes, but also my heart clean and shining as I recognize the transforming Presence of God within."

97

And now to the ironing and a prayer for each one whose garment I ironed. "I bless each garment that I iron. It is made of Spiritual Substance in the form of fabric. I smooth each garment lovingly and carefully as I let my life become smooth and free from wrinkles. I let the Love of God iron them out of me as I iron the cloth. I bless each garment and lovingly pray for the one who will wear it."

The moments fairly flew with no sense of fatigue. Where formerly the household tasks had seemed never-ending, now they were completed in half the time.

I was even able to enjoy a little time in the garden that day, to say to the plants as I lovingly watered them, "God is making you grow. Little plants, you start from a tiny seed and burst into manifestation like the ideas I plant in my mind. You grow and flourish because of the wonderful Life within you. I let the Love of God flow through me to help you grow. I bless you, for you are God as Beauty in my life."

Not one thing I had done during the entire day had seemed to be drudgery. I actually felt renewed at the end of the day.

I started the car to pick up my family. Here, too, was an opportunity to recognize the Presence and Power of God. I thought, "As I turn the key in the ignition, I recognize that God is the only Power in my life and that It is ever ready to bless me. The Infinite Power of God motivates my car and all of Life. God Intelligence directs this car, and I am protected always."

Wondrous are the workings of the Lord, and past all understanding. Mary and Martha had made peace in my life and I felt a sense of rest and calm such as I had never known.

Try bringing God into your work, not necessarily in my words but in the words and thoughts that come to you. Try blessing your work and it will bless you. Try sitting at the Master's feet with Mary, and Martha's work will be done easily and joyously in half of the time. You'll find you aren't hurried or tired any more. You'll feel you have time to live.

CHAPTER

16

THE ANGEL WATCH

For he shall give his angels charge over thee, to keep thee in all thy ways.

—Ps. 91:11

I could not pray. My prayer well had gone dry. Could this be happening to me? Over the years, I had prayed for so many and with such dauntless faith. And now, in my own hour of need, I had come to a stone wall. Where was my faith? I tried saying the Twenty-third Psalm. *The Lord is my shepherd.* That was as far as I could remember. Where were all of the promises I had, like Mary, hidden in my heart? All I could see was that ashen face, the little body that lay in the Emergency Ward. No word had come forth for hours. And still I waited. Where was my faith?

"Oh, God, I surrender this problem to you! Words do not come. Give me your faith."

And he shall give his angels charge over thee, to keep thee in all thy ways.[1]

I could not remember the rest of the psalm, but these words kept coming to me. Over and over, they were spoken in my mind. *And he shall give his angels charge over thee, to keep thee in all thy ways.* And then I got the message. The angels were watching over my dear one to keep her in all her ways. All during that long night, the longest I have ever known, I pictured those angels keeping the watch, one on each side of the bed. They were tall and filled with light. Their light filled the room. Even the bed glowed with a soft, warm light. I kept picturing the angels and that lovely light, and a great feeling of peace came over me. I did not need to keep the vigil. The angel watch was there. They were doing it for me. I could release her to their loving care. What a wonderful, comforting thought it was. He had sent His angels and they were in charge. Finally, the morning came. I washed my face and combed my hair and presented myself at the door marked "Intensive Care." I was not afraid. At last I was admitted and directed to the bedside I had visualized all during the night. A miracle had taken place. Life had returned. The angels had kept the watch and all was well. *Wondrous are the workings of the Lord and past all finding out.*

1. Ps. 91:11.

He had sent His angels at a time of great need when of myself I could do nothing. Maybe it was better that way. My own intellectualizing of the Truth in the situation would have been a poor substitute for the peace I felt in leaving my loved one to the angels.

Yes, God has many ways to bless us, and if you ever come to the place where your faith has seemingly disappeared, I recommend the angel watch. It doesn't matter whether or not they have wings. The consciousness they represent is from the Holy Spirit. You can never tell me otherwise.

For he shall give his angels charge over thee, to keep thee in all thy ways.

They can go where we cannot go, these heavenly messengers, even through locked doors and stone walls. They are there, and when all else fails, they will go to work for us. Did they not appear in the Bible to Mary when she was greatly troubled? To Daniel in the lion's den? To Peter in prison? And again in the midst of the storm, when it seemed that surely the ship would be wrecked, the angel appeared to Paul. Oh, I know just how Paul felt when he said:

For there stood by me this night the angel of God, whose I am, and whom I serve.[2]

MEDITATION

How sweet to think we do have guardian angels, God's messengers of thought ever watching over

2. Acts 27:23.

us! Angels are God's ideas ever being communicated to man. Angels are God's link with man. God's angel thoughts are a very real experience in the mind of man. If you would know more angels intimately, say to the self:

I will let God's angel thoughts speak to me today. I will trust these angel thoughts to keep me in the way that I should go, guarding and protecting me at all times. Yes, *they shall bear me up lest I dash my foot against a stone.* They shall protect me in heavy traffic, keep me immune from all disease, free me from all thoughts of lack or fear, confusion or dissension. God's angel thoughts guard and protect me each step of the way. I am never alone. Like Paul, they come to me even in prison. They open my prison of doubt and fear and set me free. They are clothed with shining "garments" (thoughts) of joy and enthusiasm. They bring me Inspiration. Ideas that are straight from the divine Mind. They are my liberators, my eternal guardians and companions. I invite God's angel thoughts to keep me in all of my ways.

And so it is.

17

SLAYING THOSE DRAGONS

*Ye are of God, little children, and have overcome
them: because greater is he that is in you, than he that
is in the world.*

—1 John 4:4

Down through the centuries in Christian mythology,
the dragon has stood for evil: *And he* [the angel of God]
*laid hold on the dragon, that old serpent, which is the Devil,
and Satan, and bound him a thousand years.*[1] The Psalmist
tells us that *those who dwell in the secret place of the Most
High shall trample the dragon under their feet.*[2] "Feet"
stand for one's understanding—that which we stand
upon spiritually. Now, if we look up the many refer-
ences in the Bible to dragons, it all begins to make
sense.

1. Rev. 20:2.
2. Ps. 91:13.

Remember the knights of old? Their first concern was to slay the dragon. We find St. George pictured in legendary art with a spear through the dragon and his foot on its neck.

Sometimes it is helpful in our own lives to impersonalize the dragons that threaten to destroy us. What are the dragons in your life? I guess we all have some. Usually we keep them locked up in the dark recesses of the mind, afraid to look at them, lest they overcome us, terrifying us into submission by their frightening appearance. Symbolically, they lash their tails at us; fire erupts from their mouths that open so wide they do seem like the "jaws of hell."

Now is the time to go out with St. George and slay the dragons before they do us harm—slay them with the sword of Truth until they are quite dead.

Let us ask ourselves: "What dragons am I hiding from myself and the world?" Anxiety is a dragon that must be slain; fears of all kinds can grow into dragons of alarming proportions. Fear of lack is a common dragon; fear of death; fear of illness; fear of people; fear of old memories that must be kept submerged because they are too terrible to look upon; fear of old age; fear of war; fear of crime; fear of enemies; and a thousand more that rear their ugly heads and hiss at us. The more we think of it, they are well named dragons.

Somehow, calling them dragons has taken them out of the closeness of personal identification. They don't belong to us anymore. We don't have to hide them away. We can let them out of the dark caves of the subconscious mind and literally trample them underfoot.

The knights of the round table had to be pure of heart in order to kill the dragon. We, too, must be pure of heart (consciousness) to overcome the dragons we have harbored within ourselves. *The pure in heart see only God [Good].* Steadfastly beholding Good, no evil can come near us. We are given Power over it.

This is the year we kill the dragon, kill all the dragons! Make a game of it. "Down goes another dragon! Never again can that old fear frighten me! I have put the sword through its neck! My foot is upon it! I am the victor, the killer of dragons, and nothing can frighten me anymore."

A MEDITATION FOR OVERCOMING DRAGONS
(From the 91st Psalm)

He that dwelleth in the secret place of the most high shall abide under the shadow of the Almighty. . . .
To abide is to remain steadfast, never wavering. Here in that secret place within, no harm can come to us. It is a secret place of refuge—that *most High consciousness* where only Truth abides.

I will say of the Lord, He is my refuge and my fortress: My God; in him will I trust. . . .
Who has not longed to be hidden, out of harm's way, behind a fortress of Truth? Secure, we can

say: *In Him will I trust.* No danger can catch us unaware when we trust, no subtle snare, no sickness or disaster has power over those who trust in Him. No evil can sneak up from the hidden recesses of our own thinking, no harm can come upon us from without unless we give it room within our thinking. It finds no room where Truth abides.

A thousand shall fall at thy side, and ten thousand at thy right hand; but it shall not come nigh thee, for only with thine eyes shalt thou behold and see the reward of the wicked.

Yes, there may still be wars and rumors of wars for those who refuse the sanctuary of the most High, but they do not come nigh us. We see the smoke in the distance, but do not smell the fire. We are not involved emotionally in that which finds no counterpart within.

There shall no evil befall thee, neither shall any plague come nigh thy dwelling.

Fear finds no place in the consciousness of the most High, for love casts it out before it can enter. Angel thoughts stand guard at our mind's door, and we are lifted up before we can stumble upon some stone of human logic. They keep us in all our ways, and we are unafraid.

And so it is.

18

TRUTH IS SOMETIMES SALTY

Let your speech be always with grace, seasoned with salt, that ye may know how ye ought to answer every man.

—Col. 4:6

"For some time I have been dealing with a man, in a business way, who does not seem to be honest. Everything in me cries out that I should sever this connection, but I am trying to see the good in this man and do not wish to judge him. Where does one draw the line?" writes a woman who seems to be caught up in a popular misconception.

PRINCIPLE IS IMPERSONAL

There is only one right way, the God way. When a person prays for Guidance, he must be willing to listen; to follow that Guidance if he would have his footsteps *directed by the Lord.*[1] Principle is impersonal. Divine right action does not protect personality. The person who seeks to be divinely guided in all that he does will receive Guidance. The one who accepts divine Protection from within will have the way revealed to him. Oftentimes, he will have prescience, the gift of seeing into the future. Through Guidance, he is able to choose the way of divine right action, avoiding the pitfalls of confused action, unloving action, and all association with misled or destructive human personalities. To be so guided is a gift from heaven. There is nothing negative about this.

THE GIFT OF PRESCIENCE

Jesus had the gift of prescience. Because he was able to see what was to come, he protected himself and those around him on several occasions. At times, he was able to bypass certain areas for his protection; he was warned to disappear in the midst of those who sought to harm him. He was protected because he walked and talked with God continually. *For Jesus knew*

1. Prov. 16:9.

from the beginning who they were that believed not, and who should betray him . . . therefore he said, *Ye are not all clean.*[2]

Another time, when Jesus and the disciples were going to Jerusalem, they were amazed when he *began to tell them what things should happen unto him.*[3]

Today, when a person has prescience and is able to point out certain business arrangements that are not in accord with Truth, he is sometimes accused of being negative, of looking at evil, or judging another person. But we were told by the great teacher that we should go and do likewise. He said, *The Father that dwells in me doeth the works . . . truly, truly, I say to you, he who believes in me will also do the works that I do; and greater works than these will he do, because I go to the Father.*[4] Because he went to the infinite Intelligence within him which he so aptly named "Father," he was guided and directed in all that he did. The works of the indwelling Father include direct Guidance from within for all who will listen and follow that Guidance. To look at evil and gloss it over by calling it good is to compromise with the enemy. On the other hand, to be warned of approaching danger is to be able to meet it in Truth without fear.

There are times when the still, small voice will whisper within, "This is not for you." There are other

2. John 6:64; 13:11.
3. Mark 10:32.
4. John 14:10,12.

times when it will seem to shout to gain attention. I know a man who heard a voice shout, "Stop the car!" He stopped just in time to avoid an oncoming truck bearing down upon him at terrific speed. Afterward, he realized that it was not a human voice that he had heard, for no person was near. The Presence of God had protected him.

CONTINUAL GUIDANCE

Those who put their faith in God, trusting not in personality, are guided continually. They know moment by moment when a person is speaking Truth. They know at once when a person is letting God act through him or whether he is acting out of fear, thinking he must use trickery to protect that which is not his by right of consciousness. There is nothing negative in seeing error for the lie that it is and standing straight and tall for Truth. As Jesus said on another occasion to those who would not listen to him:

> *Why do ye not understand my speech? Even because ye cannot hear my word. Ye are of your father the devil, and the lusts of your father ye will do. He was a murderer from the beginning, and abode not in the truth, because there is no truth in him. When he speaketh a lie, he speaketh of his own: for he is a liar, and the father of it.*[5]

5. John 8:43,44.

Jesus saw evil for what it was, the lie, *and the father of it*. Each lie, each bit of untruth, fathers further untruth, until error is compounded into utter confusion. There is no virtue in trying to make peace with error. All Power is given to Truth.

Later, as he was preparing the disciples for his departure from them, promising that the Truth would remain with them and guide them continually, he said:

> *Howbeit when he, the Spirit of truth, is come, he will guide you into all truth: for he shall not speak of himself; but whatsoever he shall hear, that shall he speak; and he will show you things to come.*[6]

The key, then, is to live according to Truth, following one's Guidance, letting the chips fall where they may. If we act in Truth, with love in our hearts, it is impossible to hurt another. Our very stand for Truth may be the thing that reveals to him that there is a better way to live. By the same token, as long as we compromise with error in the mistaken notion that we are "seeing the good in another," we are keeping that person in bondage.

Truth is impersonal, but it is sharper than a two-edged sword. It may seem to destroy the one who is not in alignment with Truth, but being impersonal, it is only severing that which is not the Truth about that person. We must be willing to trust Truth all the way in order that it may act through us. We must let Truth

6. John 16:13.

speak through us as we are guided from within, meeting error fearlessly wherever we find it, exposing it for what it is—a false prophet. It may seem unloving to those who do not understand, but Truth's way is always the loving way in the last analysis. It was Paul who said, *For the word of God is quick and powerful, and sharper than any two-edged sword, piercing even to the dividing asunder of soul and spirit, and of the joints and marrow, and is a discerner of the thoughts and intents of the heart.*[7]

TAKING A STAND

It has been said, "A man is known by the company he keeps." To associate with those who are not honest, to let them take advantage of us because we are afraid to stand for what we believe in, is to identify with their thinking; and, what is worse, it leads to silent struggle that is infinitely more destructive than an open, honest stand for the right, as God gives us to see the right.

To take a stand for Truth does not mean that we must resent people or struggle with negative situations. The key is to impersonalize. Error is neither person, place, or thing. Realizing this, we take the sting out of personality. The first and great commandment is *Him only shalt thou serve.*[8] Serving personality is not necessarily serving God. We must face every situation fairly

7. Heb. 4:12.
8. Luke 4:8.

and squarely, with complete honesty in our motives, without becoming emotionally embroiled in it.

The woman who feared to take a stand in a business transaction lest she judge another should meet her problem in this way: She should know for herself that evil is neither person, place, nor thing; that it is nothing pretending to be something. She should say to herself:

> I am not afraid of evil. It cannot interfere with the right action of God within me and within every part of life. If error is using my business associate, I know that it is not the Truth about him. I love the sinner but I abhor the sin. I do not compromise with that which is not according to Principle.
>
> As I trust my inner Guidance, I am led, guided, and directed to take the proper steps in the unfoldment of divine right action in my life and affairs. I need not placate nor appease personality but follow my Guidance fearlessly. I need not struggle to appease human thinking as I follow the straight and narrow way of Truth. The spirit of Truth within reveals to me all that I need to know. My guidance is for me. I need not convince anyone else that I am right. Nor can I judge another's growth or be responsible for the path that he should take.
>
> Cleaving to infinite Goodness, I release each and every person to his own good. Divine Intelligence makes no mistakes. As I listen to my inner Guide, I am never afraid. Only good goes from me, only Truth has place in my life. I commit my way unto the divine Law and know that my steps are ordered of the Lord.

LOVE IS PROTECTION

We know that Love is the only reality and that spiritual man is created in the image of God (Love). When all have come to this awareness, we will need no armies, we will need no courts of law. This is the millennium of which the Bible speaks. When the lion shall have lain down with the lamb, we shall not need to keep the lion in a cage. Meantime, we are living in this world that knows the ways of human laws and thinking. As Jesus said, *we must render unto Caesar that which is Caesar's and render unto God that which is God's.*[9] Out of our awareness of the perfect heaven within, we are protected in our dealings with the sometimes erring human mind.

Sometimes the road is smooth; sometimes the road is bumpy. We take it as a matter of course. We do not feel guilty when we come to a hole in the road. Our Guidance warns us to step around it. With a "Thank you, Father," we step around. We should feel just as impersonal when our Guidance warns us, "This personality is not for you." All have not yet come to their Christ awareness; some work for Caesar. There is no sin in being discriminating in our dealings with people. Some we are to walk around; with some we must be firm. Some are not for us at all. We do not have to make them over. We do not have to make them think as we do. We know them as sons of God who are not

9. Luke 20:25.

115

yet aware of their sonship. We bless them and let them go.

THE RIGHT TO CHOOSE

Each one is given the right to choose. There is no conflict in trusting and following divine Guidance, even when it seems to offend personality. It is never wrong to speak the Truth if we have been given the green light from within to do so. It is imperative that we behold the Christ in everyone, especially those in whom it seems hard to see the Christ, but there our responsibility ends. We need not look at seeming evil and call it good. We must not contribute to another's delinquency by giving encouragement to the erroneous thinking that may temporarily be using his personality.

Let your speech be always with grace [illimitable Love], *seasoned with salt* [the Truth], *that ye may know how ye ought to answer every man.*[10] In this way, we know when to speak and when to keep silent. We know when we have been warned to step around a hole in the road. We do not become emotional about the hole in the road. We do not say, "Where has my thinking been wrong that there is this hole in the road?" No, it is just another hole in the road. Thank you, Father, for protecting us always.

10. Col. 4:6.

19

ON DOING THE IMPOSSIBLE

With men this is impossible; but with God all things are possible.

—Matt. 19:26

Here is a true story of how one woman overcame a series of problems in a very effective way. I'll let her tell you in her own words.

Now I knew the meaning of frustration. For some reason we had reached an impasse, not only in one area but in several projects. Why should this happen to a couple of positive thinkers? I reasoned. It just can't be—why should we keep running down those dead-end streets, bumping our heads against stone walls?

There must be an answer, I thought. There must be a way to break the log jam.

It came to me to make a list, not of the problems facing us, but a list of the possible answers. After all, we'd gone around in circles looking at the problems long enough. From now on we'd look at answers. *With men it is impossible*, I reasoned, *but not with God: for with God all things are possible.*[1]

And so I started out on a new tack based on those powerful, affirmative words from Paul's letter to the Corinthians, *And God is able to make all Grace abound toward you; that ye, always having all sufficiency in all things, may abound to every good work.*[2]

GOD IS ABLE

I headed my list with the words: GOD IS ABLE. We were leaving the *with man this is impossible* approach and entering the realm of divine right action. My first item on the list was: The washing machine works perfectly and we are charged a fair price for the service call—*God is able.* This was a new approach entirely. The washing machine hadn't worked for some time. The repair shop had sent a "green" boy to work on it. He'd worked, all right, for hours at a time. The trouble was he didn't know what to do. We decided he'd never seen a washing machine before. And now we had a bill of $81.00 and the machine still wouldn't work. We'd telephoned the repair shop again and again and nothing seemed to make a dent in this stone wall. Impossible? It seemed that way in the long night-time hours when I mentally argued with the service

1. Mark 10:27.
2. 2 Cor. 9:8.

manager. Now we'd give God a chance. I released the problem completely with: *God is able*. What a relief! I didn't have *that* cul-de-sac to struggle with any more.

The next seemingly insurmountable problem was the water softener. Someone had told us that the dishwasher would work better if we had soft water. And so we had ordered the soft water service. It was duly installed and the bills came in, but no soft water. We had called the company. A man had come out with a testing kit and admitted we were getting no soft water. In fact, he said that the water was harder than before! We didn't think we should pay the bills but their bookkeeping department thought we should. We were tired of arguing. Thus, my next item on the list was right action regarding the water softener: *God is able*. Another load off my back. I felt lighter already.

Now I could look at what seemed an even more difficult problem—the car. We'd contracted for a new car and this involved selling the old car. We had advertised it to no avail. We added new tires and had it detailed, which I learned meant cleaning the motor and polishing the body to make it just like a new car. We spared no expense to put that automobile into first-class condition. Still, it seemed, nobody wanted it at any price. So I broke through the impasse and boldly added to my list: The car is sold at a fair price to all: *God is able*.

The next two items had to do with real estate, the kind of real estate that is supposed to be hard to sell. One piece was income property commonly known as a fixer-upper. We'd been fixing it up for years, a constant drain financially and time-wise, but it looked its age and, I suppose, because we were ready to be through with it, it was hard to believe that anyone else would want it either. We'd just had an offer that had fallen through and, frankly, our faith was at low ebb. Down on the list it went: The property is sold at the right price with the right terms for all: *God is able.* Whew! That was a relief!

The big challenge I had saved for the last item on my list, probably because I needed to build my faith before I could believe that even the omnipotent Power could help us there. Hadn't we prayed for years to sell the old house we had inherited? It, too, was a constant financial drain. If it wasn't the roof, it was the plumbing. And how we had worked on it to make it saleable! It was now in tip-top condition but the real estate people told us that nothing would sell in that area. All right. It was impossible to *us*, but *not to God.* Whatever had been said was man's opinion. To God *nothing is impossible.* Here again, *God is able.* With fresh resolve, I added this, too, to my list. The house is sold at a good price to just the right person who will love it: *God is able.*

Now it was done. I had cast my burdens on the Lord and just like the old hymn promised, I had a song in my heart and a great sense of relief. I no longer had to wake up in the middle of the night and struggle with these seemingly insurmountable problems. They weren't problems any more. By recognizing the Power of God in the midst of them I was asking in the name and nature of the Christ: *if ye ask anything in my name I will do it.* My spirit mounted up as if it had wings. The evidence hadn't appeared on the horizon, but *faith is the evidence of things not seen*, and I could rest easily now.

What happened next was just like a miracle. Even I who had seen how God works so many times before was astounded at the rapidity of our answers. The very first day a new repair man came out and fixed the washing machine. He put in new parts and did not charge us for them, nor for his work, and when we got the bill it had been reduced to what we considered a fair amount.

A few days later, the soft water service company sent their representative out to see us. He was most cooperative, and said that if we were not completely satisfied there would be no charge for the work that had been done. Thus ended that episode.

Like the invisible wind in the trees, the Power could not be seen but we could feel it working and see the effects in our lives.

Before the week was out we had sold the car for a fair price to a very nice couple, a pleasant transaction for all concerned.

By now we were not in the least surprised to have an offer for our income property, a good offer at a fair price by a very reliable party.

There remained "the big one," the *pièce de résistance* for which we had prayed so diligently, the selling of the old house. This one took another week, but when it happened it was all so effortless, so perfect in every respect, that we knew that the hand of God was in this, too. Now the list was complete, all of the problems that had seemed so difficult had been met, and we wondered why we had ever thought them difficult in the first place. *Next* time, we'll remember that *God is able* before it becomes a problem.

"GOD IS ABLE" IS THE KEY

When something works so well, the temptation is to use it as a magic incantation, a spiritual panacea for all ills, but we must ask ourselves what the basic Truth is here. Why is the *God is able* approach so effective? It works because it is sound. It is what Emmet Fox called "using the Golden Key," for it provides a successful way of taking the attention away from the condition and focusing it on God instead. Remember, Emmet Fox said: "All that you have to do is this: Stop thinking about the difficulty, whatever it is, and think about God instead." He had found that it made no difference whether the problem was big or little; whether it concerned health, finance, a lawsuit, a quarrel, an accident, or anything else conceivable. If you doubt this, give it a try.

I, too, have found that starting with *God is able* is the perfect way to get out of the *with man this is impossible* state of mind. If *God is able*, and God is right where we are—within, around, surrounding us—then, what are we worrying about? Once we have shifted the responsibility to the Wonder-working Power, we are ready to live by Grace.

I am reminded of the disciples who asked Jesus about

the man who was blind since birth, *Who did sin, this man or his parents that he was born blind?*

Jesus replied, *Neither hath this man sinned, nor his parents: but that the works of God should be made manifest in him.*[3]

When we are faced with challenges, let's not waste time berating ourselves: "Where was my thinking wrong? Why did this thing have to happen?" etc., etc. The better way is to bless the situation for good and try the *God is able* plan, that the works of God may be made manifest through us.

3. John 9:1–3.

20

FIVE MINUTES MORE

But let patience have her perfect work, that ye may be perfect and entire, wanting nothing.

—James 1:4

A delusion is a false belief, a mental misconception. Any sense of duality is a form of delusion. Every time we think of ourselves or of another person as sick, sinful, suffering or lacking, we are being deluded by a belief in duality.

There is, in Reality, One Life—a Life that is perfect. Man is the image and likeness of perfect Life. Thus, when we see imperfect man, we are experiencing a sort of double vision, or delusion. Spiritual man remains unchanging, perfect as the Father in heaven is perfect. Eternal means changeless. Spiritual man is eternal, changeless perfection.

Do you think that you see a person who is ill? Ask yourself, "Does God suffer?" Then how can God's image and likeness suffer? The perfect image, man, is one with his Source. He has never been contaminated with the delusion of sickness. Two cannot remain where there is One. The delusion must go with the realization of Truth.

Then shall two be in the field; the one shall be taken and the other left.[1] There is only one, God's man, the individualization of Spirit. There may seem to be two in the field; but, when the Lord, the divine Law operating through an awareness of eternal Truth, comes (to our awareness), it is that perfect man who remains, the son of God, made in the image and likeness of God, sinless, deathless, and birthless. Spiritual man is perfect even as the Father in heaven is perfect. An awareness of this everlasting Truth brings healing. The delusion of sickness and suffering cannot endure where there is an awareness of God.

Let us, then, be done with the delusion of duality. Do you know someone who is cantankerous, difficult to get along with? Lift the veil of false appearances and behold the loving Christ, serene, at peace with all of Life. Do you see, in passing, a hopeless cripple? Know that this is but an experience that this person is meeting. This condition is no more the Truth about him than the black cloud is the Truth about the sun. Only the Christ of God is true. See him as he truly is, even

1. Matt. 24:40.

for a moment, and he will be lifted up in his eternal experience. In this way, we are all angels unaware. Who knows the good we accomplish along life's pathway! We cannot always follow the one whom we have blessed in this manner; but, oh! the blessings we, ourselves, receive as we cleanse our own thinking from duality! At the end of a day spent saluting the Christ in all, we are cleansed, at peace with Life, and this is our reward.

Do you sometimes feel that you have failed? All of us are tempted, at times, to take this dismal detour that leads us to the pit of despair. At such times, we must remember that criticizing ourselves is judging the image and likeness of God. Every time we blame ourselves for past failures, we are looking back at the delusion of duality. Every time we find fault with the body, we are denying that it is the temple of the living God. Every time we claim a poor memory for ourselves, we are limiting the infinite Intelligence that would live through us, expressing as perfect memory. When we are tempted to sink into the slough of despondency, let us remember these beautiful words:

Behold what manner of love the Father hath bestowed upon us, that we should be called the sons of God.[2]

Somewhere along the line, we were taught to demean the self; somewhere we picked up the idea that it was virtuous to discredit ourselves.

All men have sinned, said Paul. Yes, we have all missed

2. 1 John 3:1.

the mark. But this does not mean that we should castigate ourselves. This is the sin. It is missing the mark (that is what the word *sin* actually means), it is missing what Paul called the goal of the high calling—that we should be *children of God: And, if children, then heirs, heirs of God.*[3] When we are tempted to berate ourselves, we should lift ourselves by our spiritual bootstraps, claiming our true identity. Jesus himself reminded us, *Is it not written in your law, I said, ye are Gods?*[4] We are of God; we belong to God. Dare to claim for yourself:

I am a divine, perfect, spiritual being.
My body is the temple of the living God.
My mind is the inlet and the outlet of the Mind of
  God.
I live; yet not I, but Christ lives in me.[5]

When you get up in the morning, breathe deeply before your open window as you salute the day:

MEDITATION

I greet today fearlessly; love has gone before me to prepare the way. I greet today confidently, knowing that divine Intelligence expresses through

3. Rom. 8:16, 17.
4. John 10:34.
5. Gal. 2:20.

me. I embrace this day lovingly, for only love goes from me and love returns to me. God is loving me through everyone I meet this day. I can afford to be patient and kind. I face today joyously. I am one with all of life.

And so it is.

FIVE MINUTES MORE

There is an old saying applicable to those who become discouraged when their prayers go unanswered: "Just five minutes more!"

We have all had the experience of praying and praying when no answer seems to come and we are inclined to wonder if we have just been kidding ourselves. Does He who never slumbers nor sleeps still keep watch over us?

At such a time, it takes more faith. This is the faith that turns the tide. This is the faith that causes us to finally surrender to the Power to which nothing is impossible. Then there are signs following. Now we must know with James: *Let patience have her perfect work, that ye may be perfect and entire, wanting nothing. . . . Behold we count them happy which endure.*[6]

A woman known and loved by many told me this story:

6. James 1:4; 5:11.

128

We think of Carrie Jacobs Bond as a great success, but I remember when Carrie lived in the slums in Chicago. Years ago I took her a box of groceries knowing she had nothing to eat in the house. I sat on an upturned apple box, the only piece of furniture left except the piano. We visited for awhile and then Carrie went to her piano and played the beautiful song "I Love You Truly." When she had finished there were tears in my eyes. I could see by the light in her face that she hadn't given up—she was trusting "five minutes more."

Not long after, her songs "I Love You Truly," and "The End of a Perfect Day" were on everyone's lips, the music on everyone's piano. In those days we didn't have television; we didn't even have radio at that time, but everyone knew and loved Carrie Jacobs Bond, whose fortune had changed overnight. She had so much to give and because she kept the faith for "five minutes more," her beautiful music and inspiring words helped others to keep the faith down through the years.

When things seem to be at an impasse in your life, beware of getting caught up in cul-de-sac thinking. "It is always darkest just before the dawn" has come down to us as a saying because people found it to be true. Carrie Jacobs Bond refused to give up. Because she kept the faith, she lived like a queen the rest of her life. Out of her trust in the Wonder-working Power came the inspiration to write two all-time favorite songs.

As I was with Moses, so I will be with thee: I will not fail thee, nor forsake thee,[7] is a promise you can trust. The Wonder-working Power will be with you all the way.

MEDITATION

I am a child of God. I express God's perfect Life at my level of awareness. I am a strong, vital person. Everything I do is important to God. Infinite Intelligence is available to me in making right decisions. The strength of the Almighty is mine to draw upon. Divine Love flows freely through me to everyone I meet. I am one with all of Life. I am here on this earth that I may use the gifts of the Spirit to help my fellow man. I am a unique and wonderful individualization of Spirit. God has a plan for me and is helping me carry it out into perfect fulfillment. My life has meaning. I am important to Life. Today and every day I will hold my light high so that others along the way may be blessed and inspired to lead a fuller, richer life of divine fulfillment.

And so it is.

7. Josh. 1:5.

21

LIFE IS A MIRROR

But we all, with open face beholding as in a glass the glory of the Lord, are changed into the same image from glory to glory.

—2 Cor. 3:18

That which we behold we become. That which we behold in others in some strange way attaches itself to our experience. Mostly, we discover this the hard way. Are we resisting another? It is easy to do; but beware. Even our silent resistance is mirrored back to us, often from the very one whom we would like most to please.

The Master understood this when he advised us to love our enemies, bless them that curse us, do good to them that hate us, and pray for them which despitefully use us and persecute us, *that ye may be the children of your Father which is in heaven.*[1] Truly, it is hard to do.

1. Matt. 5:44, 45.

It is much easier to resent those who misuse us. Each time we think "This time I will get by with it"; but the price is high. When we separate ourselves from another, we seem to separate ourselves from the Father in heaven. Suddenly, we are on the outside looking in.

Do we really believe that we are one with all mankind? *Do* we? Then we must accept for ourselves in this oneness that which we are accepting for our neighbor. His defeat becomes our defeat, his victory our victory. If we understand, even in a small measure, the Truth of Being, we cannot afford to judge another. Once having fallen into the trap of human judgment, we have a moral obligation to behold the Truth about that person, to salute the God Self of him until the false picture is erased in our consciousness. In this way, we are able to reach out a hand to our neighbor. In lifting him up, we find that we lift ourselves, and roses start to bloom in the wilderness where thorns have been.

HOW TO LOVE THE SINNER BUT NOT THE SIN

It is a good plan to practice daily seeing the Christ in another. Choose someone who has seemed hard to love, someone who has seemed to be an enemy, some person who seems gross, materialistic, self-centered, un-appealing, dangerous or difficult. Now talk to him (or her) silently:

I behold the Christ in you! God is loving you now. I bless you! I praise you! I love you! Christ in me is one with Christ in you. God's perfect Life is your life now. I praise the love of God within you, making you whole and at peace forevermore.

Shall we try it for a week and reap for ourselves the rich reward of feeling that we are back in the Father's house, one with Him and one with all mankind?

Once we have agreed to let the Spirit of Truth within be our daily guide and teacher, we find that there is a continual unfolding of Truth poured out for us. We are always affirmed by the Teacher within, never condemned. Truth revealed is Truth that has already been proven in our daily experience.

Well done thou good and faithful servant; thou hast been faithful over a few things, I will make thee ruler over many things: enter thou into the joy of thy lord.[2] It is the parable of the talents all over again.

GETTING RID OF RESISTANCE

It is well to take stock now and then of what we *have* learned, for in this way we make it truly ours. This I have learned: *It is a great mistake to resist paying our bills or our taxes, for this is a shortcut to a consciousness of lack.* It is important to bless the money we spend for food, no matter how inflated the prices become. It goes to

2. Matt. 25:21.

provide for the families of those who serve us, the thousands of unseen hands that prepare the food that goes on our table.

Rejoice that the baker's children have bread at their table, for truly they are one with you. And when you buy shoes, try not to resist the price. Be glad that the shoemaker's children have shoes on their feet; your purse will soon be filled again.

Even paying our taxes can be an act of Grace. Instead of resisting the waste in government, think of your part as providing a beautiful park, helping the ones in need, feeding the hungry.

When love fills your heart, it will draw your good to you in even greater abundance so that no matter what you pay out, there will always be enough in your cupboard, beautiful things around you, and enough and to spare in your checking account.

Resistance to person, place, or things is our greatest enemy, for it separates us from the Love of God. Let nothing diminish the love in your heart, for this is your treasure. When we love, we are the children of God, for God is Love. When we are one with the Source of all Love, we cannot keep our good from pouring in in an ever-increasing abundance. We must take care not to dam the flow by allowing thoughts of resistance to spending to enter our minds. I have learned to bless each dime I spend as if I were giving it to God, for it goes, in the last analysis, to help Him feed His children. I know that as His loving partner I will always be fed. Nonresistance enables me to flow with the stream of Life.

MEDITATION

I am prosperity. The substance of wealth is within me. I seek first the kingdom of divine Good within and its right use, knowing that all that I need is added unto me.

I give freely and receive joyfully out of a sense of Abundance. I dare to give from an infinite Source. I receive my good gladly, allowing others the joy of giving. My Abundance is of God. There is no power in lack. I use God's gifts wisely and joyfully. I accept my good with confidence. I am worthy of being a child of God, and all that the Father hath is mine. I put God first in my life.

I give the first fruits to God—a tenth of all that I receive. As I tithe, I prosper. In the spirit that I give to God, God gives to me. I give freely and joyfully out of a grateful heart. I am prospered in all that I do.

And so it is.

CHAPTER

22

TEN STEPS TO FREEDOM

And ye shall know the truth and the truth shall make you free.

—John 8:32

Not all prisoners brood in jails and prisons. At some time or another we have all been incarcerated in prisons of our own making. Think it over. Sometimes our bondage is to personalities we find obnoxious; at other times, a sense of sickness or poverty causes us to struggle for release. But, the harder we struggle to be free, the more relentless our jailer always seems to become.

TEN STEPS TO FREEDOM

1. The first step toward freedom is to become quiet enough to receive the Truth that will set us free. We

must remember that the door to every seeming prison opens from the inside. To push against it only causes it to close tighter. If we panic, we are lost. Now is the time to find our inner peace. We must "go within" in order to get out. If we, in our ignorance, resist the situation or personality that causes us to feel that we are in bondage, it will resist us. We must go within to find that inner peace that is the key to release.

2. Paradoxically, we must become mentally free before the key will be available to us, the key to that door that opens only from within. We must be willing to admit that the enemies *are all in our own mental household.*[1] It is not *what is done to us* that has caused us trouble, but *our own reaction to it.*

As Kahlil Gibran so aptly put it in *The Prophet: You can only be free when even the desire of seeking freedom becomes a harness to you, and when you cease to speak of freedom as a goal and a fulfillment.* In other words, we must think of ourselves as already free, and then, as within, so without, we emerge free indeed.

3. The best way I know to become free is to *look for God in the midst of the situation.* Help is as near as the Christ within. When we are willing to seek the good in the experience, the blessing is soon seen. Then, and only then, does the Christ create the new environment, the situation we have longed for.

Ye are of God, little children, and have overcome them:

1. Matt. 10:36.

because greater is he that is in you, than he that is in the world.[2] There is no power in situations. There is no power in personalities. But God within is all-Power, able to still the troubled waters, able to do all things. Whatever the need, God is the answer. Once we have found the Peace and the Power right within the situation, we are, miraculously, free to go out and live this peace.

4. *Start out by blessing the problem.* Bless it for good. Since all things do work together for good for us, there is bound to be a blessing somewhere—some growth, some unrealized opportunity to spread our wings and fly to a new level of spiritual attainment. It will help to affirm: "This, too, is for good." Affirm it until you are willing to believe it. Enough love will overcome any difficulty on the face of the earth. The answer is to love our way out of the torture chamber we have foolishly created for ourselves. It isn't always easy, but oh! so worthwhile!

5. *This is a time for thanksgiving.* It may be the last thing you want to do, but it works like magic. Start out by giving thanks for the lesson. Give thanks for the spiritual growth that is sure to follow the overcoming. Pray with all your heart: "Father, show me what I can learn from this situation, that it may bless me." Remember Job. Although his wife kept enjoining him to *curse God and die,* still he refused to sin with his lips

2. 1 John 4:4.

but stalwartly maintained: *Though he slay me, yet will I trust in him.*[3] Because he was steadfast in his spiritual integrity, the Lord blessed Job and turned his captivity so that *the Lord blessed the latter end of Job more than his beginning.*[4]

Choose the blessing rather than the curse. There's a blessing hidden in every problem if we seek it. The greater the problem, the greater the reward.

6. *This is a time for patience. Let patience have her perfect work that ye may be perfect and entire and wanting in nothing.*[5] We can't hurry God's work. It is done in His own perfect time. Once we have completed the overcoming involved, the door will open, and that particular problem, if we have been thorough, can never hurt us again. When we are able to say, "This does not move me," we have passed the graduation test and we are free to move on to a higher class. Only the "cleanup" remains. We must rid ourselves of the last dregs, lest they poison the future.

7. *It is important to rule out any sense of resentment or self-pity, which comes from lack of trust in God.* Humanly, *we see through a glass darkly.*[6] We cannot always see the deeper working of God's law, but we must continue to trust. When the going gets rough, we have the promise:

3. Job 13:15.
4. Job 42:12.
5. James 1:4.
6. 1 Cor. 13:12.

139

Great peace have they which love Thy law: and nothing shall offend them.[7]

8. I find it helps to get my mind away from the dreary present to visualize the new experience that is waiting for me on the other side of the dungeon door. *In my new heaven within I calmly build my new earth* [outer experience].

9. *This is a time for mountain-climbing.* Those who scale the highest peaks find the most beautiful flowers of all, blooming well above the timber line. As we lift our consciousness to the higher levels, we transcend those subterranean blues and are transported to a height where the problem can no longer exist.

10. *Now we can rejoice!* Free at last, even from the memory of bondage, we can exult in our freedom.

MEDITATION

I am free! I am free! I am free with the freedom of the sons of God!

I now release all problems to Him Who is able to solve them. *The Father within doeth the works!* Oh, how beautifully He does them! I surrender my life to God and I am free at last!

7. Ps. 119:165.